Presenting the Past

2

Britain 1500–1750

Andrew Wrenn
Keith Worrall

Contents

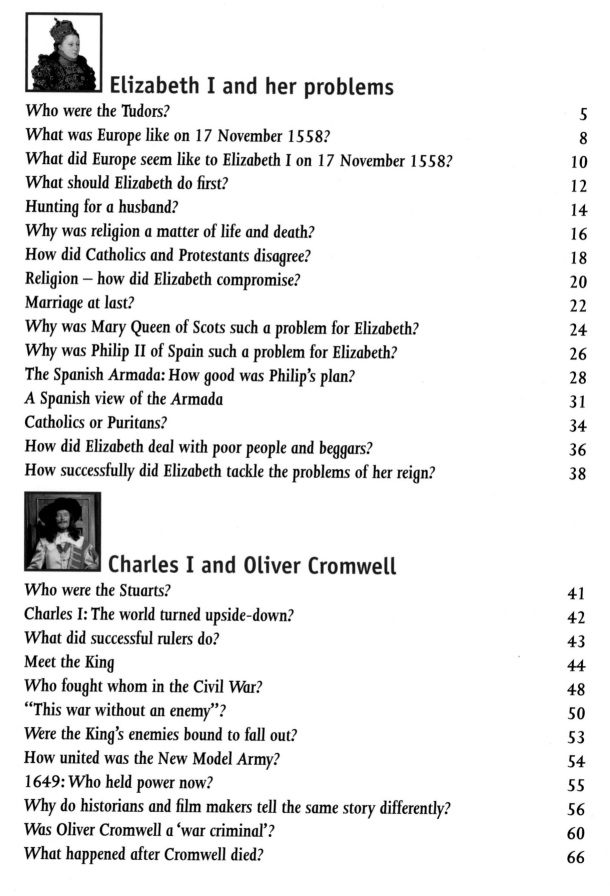

Elizabeth I and her problems

Charles I and Oliver Cromwell

How close to success did the Jacobites come?

Images of an age

Published by Collins Educational
An imprint of HarperCollinsPublishers Limited
77–85 Fulham Palace Road
Hammersmith
London
W6 8JB

www.**Collins**Education.com
On-line support for schools and colleges

20 19 18 17 16 15 14 13 12 11

ISBN 978 0 00 711461 0

Andrew Wrenn and Keith Worrall assert their moral
rights to be identified as the authors of this work.

British Library Cataloguing in Publication Data
A catalogue record for this publication is available
from the British Library.

Edited by Sue Chapple
Design by Ken Vail Graphic Design, Cambridge
Cover design by Derek Lee
Artwork by Peter Bull
Picture research by Sarah Clarke
Production by Katie Morris
Printed and bound by Printing Express Ltd.

Cover image: The Execution of Lady Jane Grey in the Tower of London in 1553,
         1833 by Hippolyte Delaroche (Paul)(1797-1856), National Gallery,
         London, UK/Bridgeman Art Library

Henry VII 1485–1509

- ◆ The first Tudor king
- ◆ Took the throne by killing Richard III at the Battle of Bosworth
- ◆ A cautious man, who ruled wisely

Henry VIII 1509–1547

- ◆ Surviving son of Henry VII
- ◆ A dangerous and ruthless ruler
- ◆ **Protested** against the power of the Pope by making his own **'Protestant'** Church in England

Edward VI 1547–1553

- ◆ Henry VIII's only son, aged nine when he became King
- ◆ The lords who ruled in his name made huge changes to bring in **Protestant** ideas

Mary I 1553–1558

- ◆ Henry VIII's oldest daughter
- ◆ A strong Catholic, she set about making England **Catholic** again

Elizabeth I 1558–1603

- ◆ Henry VIII's second daughter, a half-sister to Mary
- ◆ **What did she believe? What would she do? What would happen next?**

It is Thursday 17 November, in 1558. Elizabeth Tudor is about to be declared Queen.

I remember them all

This is Old Meg (or Smelly Old Meg, as the children call her). She was born in March 1485, which makes her 73 now, one of the oldest people in England. Meg shuffles along the busy London streets, which are filled with crowds waiting for the news to be announced. But Meg has seen it all before …

"I remember them all ..."

Old Meg walks along by the Thames.
A ship is unloading its cargo.
That reminds her ...

People knew what to believe when I was young!

> God is in heaven.
> The Earth is flat.
> The Pope is head of the Church.

Simple, really. But people can never just accept what they're told. They always have to start changing things.

My mother told me about that foreigner Christopher Columbus, who left Spain in a ship in 1492. He discovered what they called the New World — and then suddenly it turned out the world was round, not flat! Stupid idea — we'd all fall off if it was true!

That was when **Henry VII** was King. He must have been a good king because there weren't any wars and on the whole things didn't change too much.

Well, I still know what I believe ...

> God is in heaven.
> The Earth is flat.
> The Pope is head of the Church.

Anyway, let's see what Mary's sister **Elizabeth** does, now she's Queen. I wonder if she'll be any better ... ?

Things _should_ have got better under our next queen, **Mary**. She was a good Catholic and she made the Pope head of the Church again. The Protestants left the country, kept quiet, or got burned like the wood on that fire. But the monasteries were still in ruins and she married that King Philip of Spain, who dragged us into his war against France.

Prices still went up, there were even more beggars, and we were _still_ at war!

Next Meg passes a ruined monastery. People have taken some of the stones for building.

*It was that fat old **Henry VIII** who started all the real changes. Six times he married! His first wife, Catherine, was a good Catholic queen. <u>She</u> knew the Pope was head of the Church! But when she couldn't have a son, Henry wanted to get rid of her.*

The Pope said he couldn't divorce her, so what did Henry do? He listened to those wicked Protestants from Germany, like Martin Luther, who said kings should be head of the Church, not popes. Silly man. Next thing, Henry creates his own Church, divorces Catherine and marries his fancy woman, Anne Boleyn.

Everything fell apart then. Henry closed down all the monasteries like this one, so that he could take their money. Poor people like me couldn't get any help from the monks then. After a while, the Protestants even put English bibles in the churches. Prices went up and up and we always seemed to be at war. Terrible times.

*I felt sorry for that little boy king, **Edward VI**. The Protestants who advised him became even more powerful, taking ideas from a new Protestant leader in Switzerland, called John Calvin. They spread these ideas from their fancy printing presses like this one, though it was really only a few people who could read their books.*

Prices still went up, there were beggars everywhere and we were still at war.

What was Europe like on 17 November 1558?

IRELAND

SCOTLAND

ENGLAND

FRANCE

PORTUGAL

SPAIN

TURKISH EMPIRE

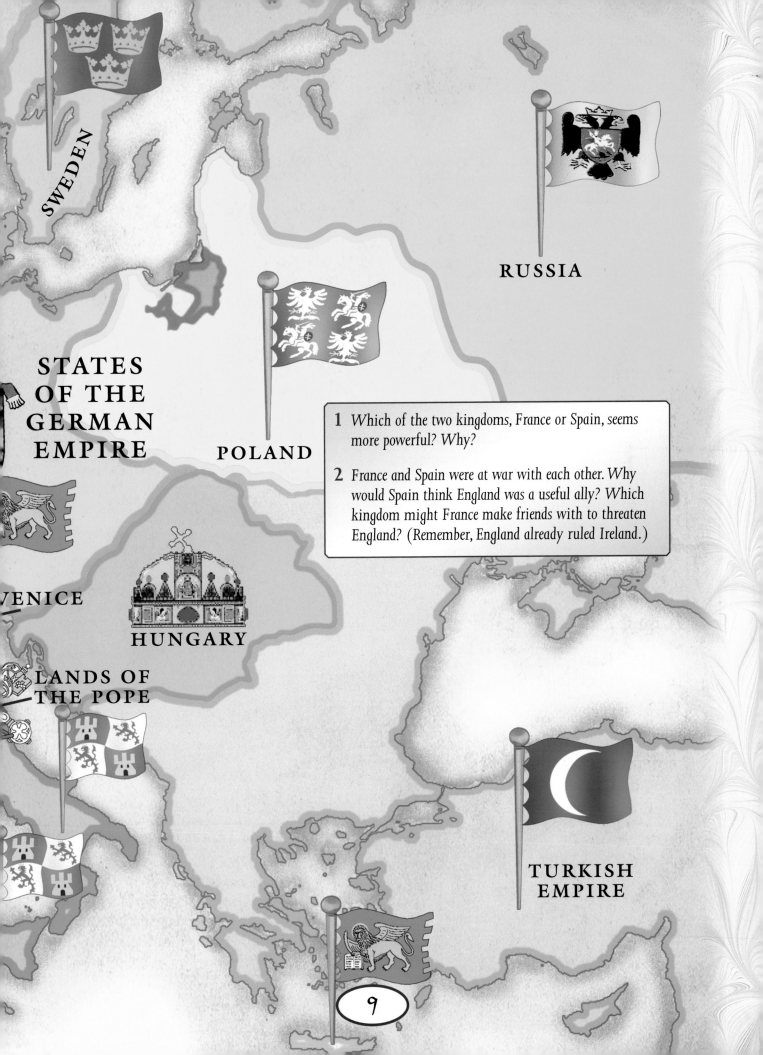

SWEDEN

RUSSIA

STATES
OF THE
GERMAN
EMPIRE

POLAND

1 Which of the two kingdoms, France or Spain, seems more powerful? Why?

2 France and Spain were at war with each other. Why would Spain think England was a useful ally? Which kingdom might France make friends with to threaten England? (Remember, England already ruled Ireland.)

VENICE

HUNGARY

LANDS OF
THE POPE

TURKISH
EMPIRE

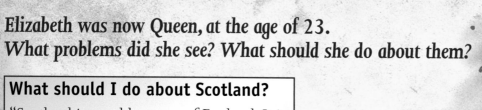

Elizabeth was now Queen, at the age of 23.
What problems did she see? What should she do about them?

What should I do about Scotland?

"Scotland is an old enemy of England. It is ruled by Catholics, led by my cousin, the young Queen Mary. They are struggling to control the people who have become Protestants in the country. French troops are in Scotland to help the Catholics."

What should I do about Ireland?

"I am Queen of Ireland, but my soldiers only control the land around Dublin. The rest of the country is run by Irish chiefs who fight each other and my soldiers."

What should I do about beggars and poor people?

"We have had bad harvests for three years in a row. It's been a better harvest this year, but still there are more and more beggars and poor people."

Should I marry and try to provide an heir?

"I need an heir who can succeed me when I die."

Edinburgh

Dublin

WALES

London

Canterbury

Calais

Paris

FRANCE

SPAIN

How should I treat my ally, King Philip?

"King Philip II of Spain also rules the Spanish Netherlands. His lands are very close to England. He is a very powerful Catholic ruler. He was my sister Mary's husband. England is now at war with France because Philip persuaded my sister that England should join him in fighting the French."

Elizabeth I on 17 November 1558?

What should I do about money?

"My sister has left me debts of £250,000. That's a huge amount of money! The war with France is costing more and more. Would Parliament give me more tax money if I asked them?"

Should I continue burning Protestants?

"My sister Mary had over 200 Protestants burnt to death. Her Catholic bishops, who are very powerful, want to carry on with this policy."

NISH
HERLANDS

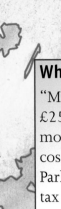

What should I do about the war with France?

"England is at war with France. We lost the town of Calais to the French this year. The young Queen of Scotland, Mary, has just married the son of the King of France. Now my sister is dead, the Queen of Scotland claims to be the true Queen of England as well. This war is costing more and more."

Should I hurry to appoint a new Archbishop of Canterbury?

"The Archbishop of Canterbury has just died. I have to appoint someone new to lead the Church. However, while there is no Archbishop of Canterbury, I get the money from his lands."

Should I obey the Pope and keep the Church Catholic?

"My sister Mary made the Pope head of the English Church. I could make myself head of my own Protestant Church of England."

Rome

As you can see, Elizabeth had many problems. What should she do about them? On the next pages you will help her sort out how to solve these problems.

What should Elizabeth do first?

This is King Henry VIII's writing desk. Perhaps Queen Elizabeth I, his daughter, began to use it. Henry may have been a role model for her. After all, he had been a strong ruler – fighting wars against France, standing up to the Pope and making himself head of the Church in England. Could Elizabeth be a strong ruler like her father?

1 Imagine that the Queen wrote out some questions to think about on slips of paper on her writing desk.

Should I hurry to appoint a new Archbishop of Canterbury?

Should I marry and try to provide an heir?

What should I do about Scotland?

Should I continue burning Protestants?

What should I do about Ireland?

What should I do about money?

What should I do about the war with France?

What should I do about poor people and beggars?

How should I treat my ally King Philip?

Should I obey the Pope and keep the Church Catholic?

2 In pairs, discuss which questions seem to belong together. Try writing out the questions on paper and arranging them in groups on your desk, as the Queen might have done. Think of different headings that the questions have in common, e.g. war, money, etc.

3 After you have made your decisions, record them like this:

"I think these two questions go together – "What should I do about the war with France?" and "What should I do about money?"

I think they go together because …"

You may find the questions can be arranged in lots of different ways. Discuss your decisions with another pair.

4 Once the Queen has organised her questions, she will have to decide which ones she will discuss with her advisers. She now needs to re-organise these questions in a new way, to prioritise them. These headings will be:

a) Questions I must make a decision about **very quickly**.

b) Questions I must make a decision about **eventually** (there's no hurry).

c) Questions **I don't need to do anything** about at all.

In a small group, decide which questions belong under which heading. Write a paragraph about each heading, to explain your decisions.

Hunting for a husband?

As well as all the political and religious questions worrying her, there was one very personal problem facing Elizabeth — should she get married? It was a very important question for her because her husband would become King and would rule with her.

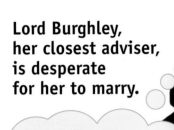

Lord Burghley, her closest adviser, is desperate for her to marry.

She can't marry that Robert Dudley — his father was a traitor.

Her Majesty __must__ marry because …

◉ *England needs a male heir.*

◉ *England needs a strong man to rule the country, and one who can command the respect of the lords.*

◉ *England needs a Protestant husband for the Queen (preferably). I'm a Protestant. If the Queen marries a Catholic, it would be a disaster.*

◉ *England doesn't want a foreigner like King Philip of Spain, who might drag the country into other people's wars again. We've only just made peace with France.*

I don't want a man to control me. __If__ I marry, I would like an attractive husband.

The Queen had her own ideas …

❀ *I shouldn't marry a foreigner (the English don't like them), especially if it drags England into foreign wars.*

❀ *I would have to be careful if I married one of the English lords, or a man linked with them. The other lords would get jealous.*

❀ *I should really marry a Protestant. After all, I'm a Protestant myself.*

❀ *I can control men better by just flirting with them — I don't need to marry.*

Lots of men wanted to marry the Queen. Who would she choose?

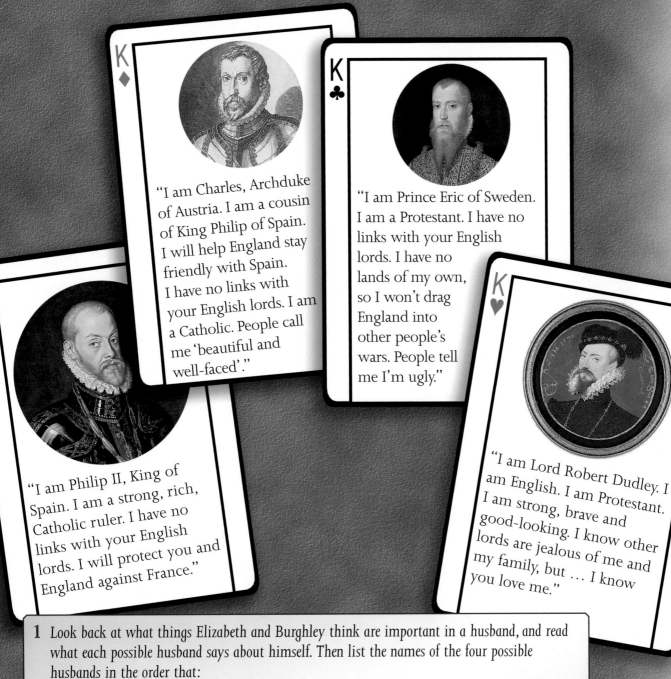

K ♦

"I am Charles, Archduke of Austria. I am a cousin of King Philip of Spain. I will help England stay friendly with Spain. I have no links with your English lords. I am a Catholic. People call me 'beautiful and well-faced'."

K ♣

"I am Prince Eric of Sweden. I am a Protestant. I have no links with your English lords. I have no lands of my own, so I won't drag England into other people's wars. People tell me I'm ugly."

K ♥

"I am Lord Robert Dudley. I am English. I am Protestant. I am strong, brave and good-looking. I know other lords are jealous of me and my family, but … I know you love me."

"I am Philip II, King of Spain. I am a strong, rich, Catholic ruler. I have no links with your English lords. I will protect you and England against France."

1 Look back at what things Elizabeth and Burghley think are important in a husband, and read what each possible husband says about himself. Then list the names of the four possible husbands in the order that:

a) Burghley probably preferred them   **b)** the Queen probably preferred them

2 How much would they have agreed and disagreed about the order?

3 From what you know about Elizabeth and the situation in England, what factors do you think she <u>should</u> take into account when deciding whether she should marry someone or not? Here are some suggestions:

◆ Country — foreign or English?   ◆ Personality — strong or weak?

◆ Looks — handsome or unattractive?   ◆ Religion — Catholic or Protestant?

◆ Wealth — very rich or less well off?

In fact, Elizabeth stayed single, although she sometimes dragged out marriage negotiations with these possible husbands if it suited her.

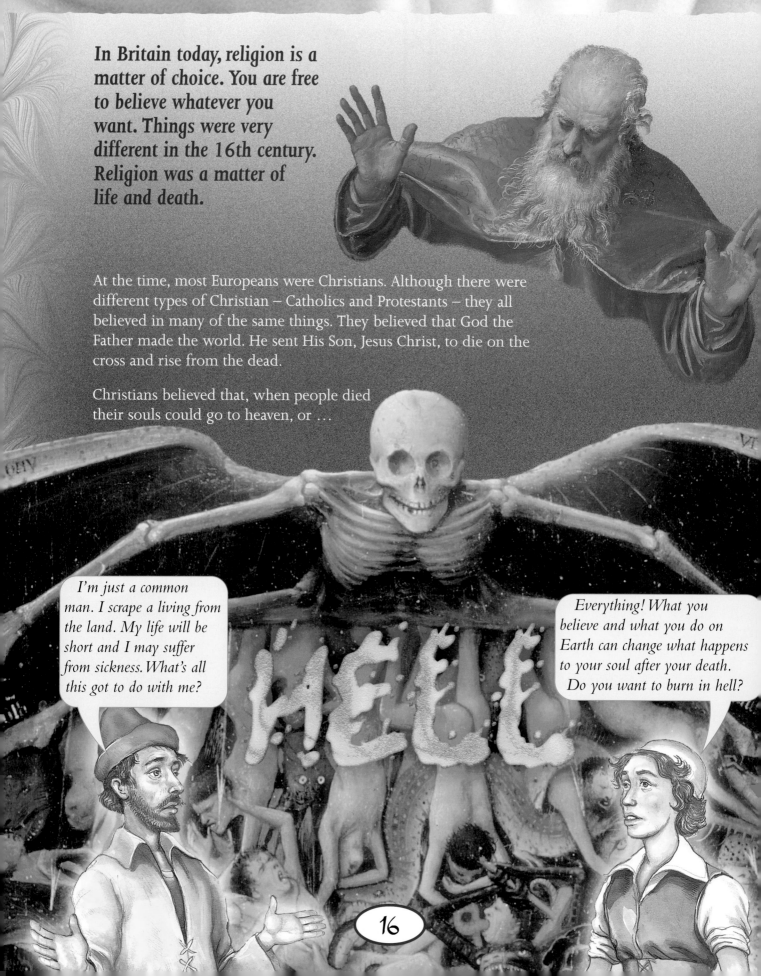

In Britain today, religion is a matter of choice. You are free to believe whatever you want. Things were very different in the 16th century. Religion was a matter of life and death.

At the time, most Europeans were Christians. Although there were different types of Christian – Catholics and Protestants – they all believed in many of the same things. They believed that God the Father made the world. He sent His Son, Jesus Christ, to die on the cross and rise from the dead.

Christians believed that, when people died their souls could go to heaven, or …

I'm just a common man. I scrape a living from the land. My life will be short and I may suffer from sickness. What's all this got to do with me?

HELL

Everything! What you believe and what you do on Earth can change what happens to your soul after your death. Do you want to burn in hell?

Religion: power to rule?

Elizabeth was crowned Queen in Westminster Abbey. She had to be crowned in a church because people believed that it was God who gave her the right to rule.

Her crown was topped by a Christian cross.

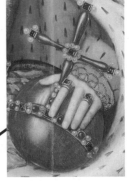

She held an orb of gold (a symbol of the world), with a Christian cross on it.

Elizabeth was powerful because everyone believed that her power came from God. God would judge her on how she used it.

A Christian ruler was directly responsible for what <u>all</u> his/her people believed. This meant that Elizabeth was responsible for everything that should be taught to the people about religion. It mattered what people in England believed because <u>she</u> might go to hell if <u>they</u> believed the wrong thing.

What difference does it make who is King or Queen? What does it matter?

How can you say that? The Queen decides what we must believe. You can be killed for believing the wrong thing.

1 Compare this with the situation in Britain today:
 ◆ Who is head of the Church of England?
 ◆ What other religions are there in modern Britain?
 ◆ What do the Queen and the Prime Minister have to do with religion?

Catholics and Protestants believed in different versions of the same broad religion.

If you were a Catholic, you believed that ...

◆ you must do what the Church teaches.

◆ souls can go to purgatory – a place of punishment between heaven and hell.

◆ the prayers of the living can help the souls of the dead to move out of purgatory and into heaven.

◆ the Church can help you to save your soul from hell.

◆ you must **confess** [admit] your **sins** [wrong thoughts and actions] to a priest, and you must pray to the Virgin Mary and the saints for help.

◆ you must go to **Mass** [a special service], where bread and wine become the body and blood of Jesus. Only priests drink the wine because it is so special.

◆ the Pope is head of the Church everywhere, getting his power directly from God. He leads the bishops and priests, who help you to communicate with God.

◆ anyone who goes against the teaching of the Church can be burned as a heretic.

If you were a Protestant, you believed that ...

◆ you must obey the Bible.

◆ purgatory is not in the Bible, therefore it does not exist.

◆ praying for dead people is wrong and a waste of time, because it's too late to help them.

◆ the Church cannot save your soul from hell. Only God can do this.

◆ only God can help you get to heaven, not your priest.

◆ in church, everyone takes bread and wine as a way of remembering Jesus. They do <u>not</u> physically change into His body and blood.

◆ the Pope is not head of the Church, and the bishops and priests are not necessary for you to communicate with God.

◆ you should follow important Protestant leaders like Martin Luther and John Calvin.

Extreme Protestants sometimes went further.

Although they were very serious and moral, they hated the way Catholics worshipped.

Smash the statues! It's wrong to worship idols.

Whitewash the pictures.

A Catholic church and a Protestant church could look very different, because of the different beliefs of Catholics and Protestants.

A Catholic church

wall paintings of Bible stories and of the saints

statue of the Virgin Mary to respect and pray in front of

place to say prayers for souls in purgatory

colourful robes which the priest wears for Mass

screen to separate off the most holy part of the church

stained glass showing Bible stories and images of saints

crucifix – Jesus on the cross

wafer and wine which become Jesus

service book in Latin

stone altar where the priest repeats the sacrifice of Jesus' death

A Protestant church

walls painted white, with no pictures

the Ten Commandments from the Bible, to remind people of God's laws

lectern for the Bible – in English so that everyone can hear and read it

no statues to worship

no screen to separate minister and people

plain glass windows, with no pictures to worship

plain cross with no statue

a plain wooden holy table

bread and wine as a symbol of Jesus

minister dressed in plain robes

1 Make a list of the main similarities and differences between a Protestant and a Catholic church.

19

Whether the country was officially Protestant or Catholic was very important. It also mattered to other countries, which would decide whether to be an ally or an enemy. Elizabeth inherited a difficult situation. In recent years, England had swung between being Protestant and Catholic.

Henry VIII, Elizabeth's father, broke away from the Pope, made himself head of his own Church, and closed the monasteries.

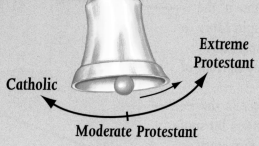

Under **Edward VI**, Elizabeth's half-brother, the Church of England became more and more Protestant, closer to the ideas of John Calvin.

Under **Mary I**, Elizabeth's half-sister, the English Church became Catholic again. Mary burnt a number of Protestants at the stake.

Everyone looked to Elizabeth, to see what she would do. What would happen next?

Both Catholics and Protestants had suffered for their beliefs at different times. Elizabeth claimed she would be different. She said "I will not make windows into men's souls". She meant she would not look too deeply into what people believed, and judge them. Under the new Queen, the laws changed.

Elizabeth …

◆ called herself supreme governor of the Church of England, not head. (She was trying to be more moderate than her father – the title 'governor' did not offend Catholics as much.)

◆ kept priests and bishops but said the Pope had no power in England.

◆ allowed <u>some</u> pictures, statues and stained glass.

◆ allowed services in English but not Latin.

◆ banned the Catholic service of Mass.

◆ allowed priests to marry.

◆ banned prayers for the dead.

A church in Elizabeth's reign

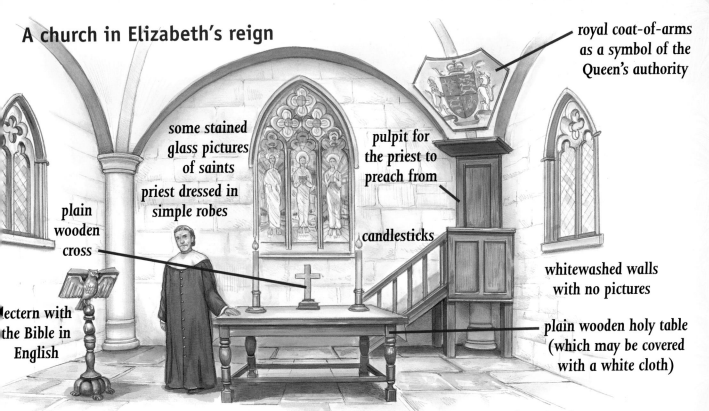

royal coat-of-arms as a symbol of the Queen's authority

some stained glass pictures of saints

pulpit for the priest to preach from

plain wooden cross

priest dressed in simple robes

candlesticks

lectern with the Bible in English

whitewashed walls with no pictures

plain wooden holy table (which may be covered with a white cloth)

Elizabeth tried to satisfy both Catholics and Protestants with her Church of England. But was she likely to succeed? Could she keep both types of Christians happy?

1 Look back at what Catholics believed and what their churches looked like. Then imagine you are an Elizabethan Catholic and write sentences starting:

As a Catholic I approve of these things about Elizabeth's Church …

However, I disapprove of these things about Elizabeth's Church …

I have mixed feelings about Elizabeth's Church because …

2 Now do the same as if you were an Elizabethan Protestant writing about Elizabeth's Church.

3 Look back at the bells which show the changing swings of religion during the reigns of Henry VIII, Edward VI and Mary I. Draw a bell for Elizabeth's reign which makes clear the changes she made to religion.

In our church we once prayed to the saints – and we had all the pictures and the Latin in King Henry's time. Then in King Edward's time the church was whitewashed and they smashed all the statues. Then in Queen Mary's time they tried to put all the statues and pictures back. Now it's all change again. What are we supposed to believe?

Just go to church and do as you're told. Ordinary people survive if we keep our heads down. Who knows, things may change again. Do you want to burn at the stake?

Marriage at last?

By 1581, Elizabeth was 48 years old. Her advisers still wanted her to marry. People thought she was still young enough to have children. Then for the first time she came very close to marriage – not because it was forced on her but because she had at last met someone she actually wanted to marry!

J ♥

- ♥ I am François, Duke of Alençon.
- ♥ I am the youngest brother of the King of France.
- ♥ I am young (26 years old), healthy and good-looking.
- ♥ I have no links with English lords.
- ♥ I am a Catholic, but I quite like Protestants.
- ♥ I am deeply and passionately in love with Elizabeth.

Look back at page 14 to remind yourself of what the Queen and Lord Burghley expected from any husband for the Queen. Can you see why she liked Alençon and why some of her advisers thought he would be suitable? She called him her "dearest frog".

However, Alençon had one big disadvantage. Many English people remembered the marriage of Elizabeth's sister Mary to Philip of Spain. They hated and feared the idea of another foreign, Catholic prince marrying an English queen.

Hands off – don't tell the Queen what to do!

John Stubbs was a Puritan lawyer (Puritans were extreme Protestants). Secretly, he wrote a pamphlet against the marriage, and then had it published. He said that:

- *Alençon was the 'scum of all France'.*
- *The French prince and his followers would be like leeches on the flesh of England.*
- *Alençon was not really interested in the Queen, because he was half her age, and would very quickly be unfaithful.*
- *The Queen might die if she had a baby, since she was now so old.*

Stubbs signed himself 'Your Majesty's loving true servant'.

The Queen was furious. She ordered Stubbs's right hand to be cut off. It took three blows. Afterwards, Stubbs tried to raise his hat with his left hand, shouted "God save the Queen", and then fainted.

In the end, Elizabeth did not marry Alençon – or anyone else.

So why <u>did</u> Elizabeth punish Stubbs? Was it because her feelings were badly hurt, or was there more to it?

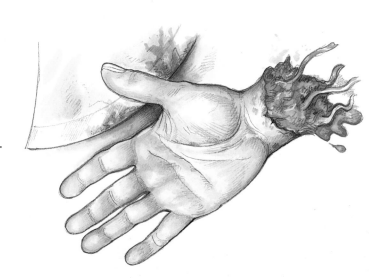

1 Look at this table. Decide whether each possible reason for punishing Stubbs was to do with:

① the Queen's personal feelings **②** a threat to her power **③** both of these

Read the background information carefully before you make your decision.

Possible reason	Background information	① ② or ③
Stubbs was a Puritan (an extreme Protestant).	Elizabeth disliked Puritans a lot and sometimes treated them harshly. Punishing one Puritan was an easy way of warning others not to cause trouble.	
Stubbs openly insulted the Queen.	Elizabeth was a woman ruler who took great care to appear strong and in control. Her image could easily be damaged. She still believed she could have children.	
Stubbs wrote about the Queen's marriage, which was forbidden by law.	Elizabeth stopped everyone debating possible marriages or who should succeed her. Some of her advisers may have encouraged Stubbs to publish his pamphlet in order to stop a foreign marriage they hated. It was a way of showing the Queen what they could not say. Her answer was to punish Stubbs.	
Stubbs insulted Alençon.	Elizabeth was probably in love with Alençon. She did not like being shown up in front of a foreign prince. An insult to Alençon was also an insult to his brother, the King of France.	

Mary Queen of Scots was Elizabeth's cousin, and a strong Catholic. In 1568, she escaped from Protestant rebels in Scotland and crossed the border into England.

Mary was confident that her cousin would help her, but Elizabeth wasn't so sure it was the right thing to do …

◆ Mary had a claim to Elizabeth's throne and was likely to become Queen of England if Elizabeth died. Many Catholics thought that she should already be Queen of England instead of Elizabeth.

◆ The rebels in Scotland were Protestants who did not want Mary back.

◆ Mary might travel to get help from Catholic France or Spain This would put England in danger.

◆ Mary was accused of the murder of her second husband, Lord Darnley.

On the one hand, Mary was a fellow queen, and a cousin On the other hand she was a dangerous Catholic rival and a possible murderer. Elizabeth decided not to offer any help. Instead, she kept Mary a prisoner for 19 years.

Yet Mary was even dangerous in prison. Fellow Catholics plotted to free her and put her on the English throne. Finally in 1586, Elizabeth's spy chief, Sir Francis Walsingham, trapped Mary into agreeing to a wild plot to assassinate Elizabeth. Mary was found guilty of treason against Elizabeth

Now what should Elizabeth do about Mary?

She had four main choices. She could:

1 **execute** Mary on a charge of treason.
2 keep Mary in **prison**
3 **free** Mary from prison to live in England
4 **exile** Mary, sending her to live in France

Hmmm, what shall I do?

---

1 Think about what might be the good and the bad results for Elizabeth of each of these choices. What do _you_ think Elizabeth should do?

Even though Mary had been found guilty of treason, Elizabeth was in no hurry to execute her. At first she refused to sign the death **warrant** [order]. She would hint in conversations that she wished someone would murder Mary, especially to save embarrassment in France and Scotland. Finally, she gave in to the pressure from her advisers.

- On 1st February 1587 she sent her secretary, Davison, to bring the warrant. He hid it in the middle of a pile of other papers, hoping that would make it easier for her to sign it.
- While she signed the papers, she chatted about the weather. She then told Davison to take the warrant to Walsingham.
- Elizabeth gave instructions that the execution should take place indoors, out of sight of the public. She was not to be told anything about it until afterwards.
- She sent a private letter to Mary's gaoler, asking him to quietly murder Mary.
- On the 8th February, Mary was executed. Elizabeth was furious. She accused her advisers of acting without her direct permission.
- She denied responsibility for Mary's death.
- She refused to see Lord Burghley for weeks, imprisoned Davison in the Tower of London and fined him £10,000, wrecking his career.
- She wore black clothes in Mary's memory and ordered a royal funeral in Peterborough Cathedral.

Sometimes there is a difference between what people say and do, and what they really think. It is difficult to know exactly what Elizabeth may have been thinking but historians have tried to guess, from what she did. You can do the same.

2 Write what Elizabeth might have been thinking on 1st February 1587.

3 Write what Elizabeth might have been thinking on 8th February 1587.

4 What do you think the reaction to Mary's execution was from:
   a) Elizabeth's <u>Protestant</u> advisers, like Burghley and Walsingham?
   b) the <u>Catholic</u> King of Spain?

5 Do <u>you</u> think Elizabeth did the right thing? Use the sentences below to help you with your answer.

I think the best option was _____, because _____

I think the worst option was _____, because _____

I think Elizabeth's decision to execute Mary was _____,
because _____

King Philip II of Spain was the most powerful Catholic ruler in Europe. From his palace in Madrid, he ruled an empire that stretched around the world. But even Philip had his problems. Imagine if we could eavesdrop on his prayers in 1587. What might he be saying ...?

Most Blessed Virgin and Mother of our Lord Jesus Christ, I, Philip, a miserable sinner, give thanks for your protection. Mother of God, I thank you again for all my victories:

◆ *for beating the French in 1557. We lost only 500 dead to their 5,000. I built this monastery and palace of San Lorenzo because we won the battle on his saint's day.*

◆ *for beating the Turks in 1571. Our ships, with the help of our Holy Father the Pope, sank about 200 of theirs. They lost 30,000 men. We lost only 10 ships and 8,000 dead. The victory saved all of Christian Europe from the Turkish Muslims.*

◆ *for the peaceful takeover of Portugal and its empire around the world in 1581. My mother was a princess of Portugal. When their last king died with no children, I took over as their new ruler. The lands of Spain and Portugal became one, to spread the gospel and the power of the one, true, Catholic Church.*

Philip collected the remains of saints to help him in his prayers. He kept them in cupboards like this. He had nearly 7,000, including ten whole bodies, 306 arms and legs, and 144 heads.

So, I beg for one more miracle. You know the evil lies of Elizabeth, so called Queen of England.

◆ *She is a Protestant heretic and an unlawful child of Henry VIII and Anne Boleyn.*

◆ *She sends soldiers and money to support the Dutch people who are fighting against me. They are Protestant heretics too.*

◆ *She sends her pirates to raid my treasure ships. She denies that she supports them but I know she is lying. She even gets a cut of the treasure.*

◆ *She punishes English Catholics with fines and prison. Worst of all, she tortures true priests like Edmund Campion to death.*

◆ *Lastly, she kept her own cousin, Mary Queen of Scots, the rightful Queen of England and Ireland, in prison for 19 years. And now I have heard she has killed Mary. So another Catholic martyr dies for the true faith.*

Holy Mother of God, you know how patient I have been with this woman. I offered to marry her when her sister died all those years ago. I protected her from the French and the anger of the Pope. I waited for her to turn back to your true Church. She cannot be trusted. Please bless my Armada and bring back the English to the true faith. Amen.

Although this prayer is made up, all the facts are correct. It is probably the kind of prayer Philip would have said. Philip did decide to send an **Armada** [fleet of ships] to fight the English.

Elizabeth and Philip saw each other as a major threat. But who was the bigger threat to whom?

---

1 In pairs, fill in a table like the one below, listing as many reasons as you can why Elizabeth and Philip were a threat to each other.

Elizabeth	Philip
Elizabeth was a threat to Philip because she ...	Philip was a threat to Elizabeth because he ...

2 Now complete this sentence:

I think _____ was the bigger threat to _____ because _____

Philip gathered as many ships as he could, to create a huge Armada which would be able to invade England. What was the plan? And what really happened?

1 The plan

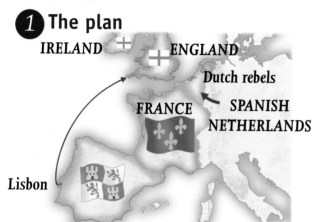

Philip would send out a huge fleet of ships from Spain, well equipped, under the command of Admiral Santa Cruz, Spain's best sailor.

1 What actually happened

Santa Cruz died before the ships even set sail. Philip replaced him with the Duke of Medina-Sidonia, but he suffered from seasickness and really didn't want the job. Meanwhile, Sir Francis Drake, Vice-Admiral of the English fleet, raided Cadiz and damaged many of the ships waiting there. The Armada of 131 ships at last set sail from Spain in May 1588 but bad weather forced it to take shelter in Corunna. Ships were damaged, food supplies low and rotting, and precious time was lost.

2

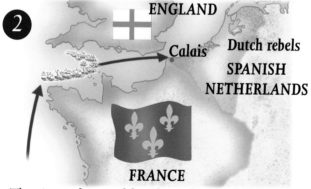

The Armada would sail up the English Channel in a crescent formation towards Calais. It was ordered not to land any troops or break its formation. The strongest ships were at the tips of the crescent, so that they could easily surround any English ship which threatened the centre.

2

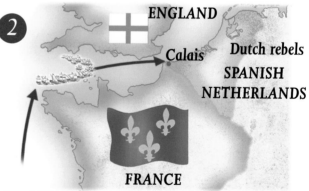

Lord Howard, Commander of the English fleet, harassed the Armada as it sailed up the Channel in August. The lighter and faster English ships picked off some stragglers but the crescent formation remained intact.

3

At Calais, the Armada would take on board the best troops of the Duke of Parma's army from the Spanish Netherlands.

4

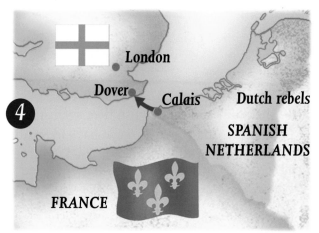

The Armada would cross to the English coast and land Parma's troops together with soldiers already on board the Armada ships.

5

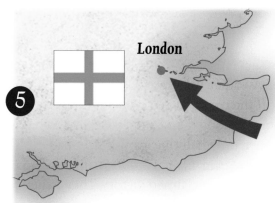

The soldiers would invade England and quickly capture London. Thousands of English Catholics would then rise up to support the Spanish against Elizabeth.

3

6th August: The Armada anchored **outside** Calais because no-one knew whether the harbour was deep enough for the Spanish ships. The Duke of Parma's troops were not ready to go on board and some were trapped by Dutch rebels.

4

7th August: The English set some old ships on fire and sent them towards the Armada. The Spanish were afraid the ships might be full of explosives (the Dutch rebels sometimes used this trick). They panicked and cut their anchors, heading out to sea. In fact, the fire ships were empty – but the crescent formation was now broken.

5

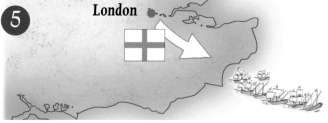

No invasion happened. No Catholics rose up. The Queen rode to Tilbury in Essex and inspired her soldiers. They were a weak and poorly-equipped army, though, and no match for Parma's crack troops. It was just as well the Spanish never landed.

6

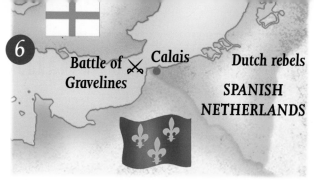

The soldiers would then go on to occupy all of England and Ireland with support from local Catholics.

8th August: the English fleet attacked the Armada and caused a lot of damage. The Spanish were poor at firing their cannons. Some of their cannonballs were even the wrong size to fit the spanish cannons! Eventually the English withdrew, tired and running out of ammunition.

7

With Elizabeth's defeat and death, Philip's daughter would become Queen of England, the Pope would be head of the English Church again, and English Catholics would be free from persecution.

With the wind and the English fleet against them, the Armada tried to escape back to Spain by sailing north around Scotland. The English ships eventually returned home. Nearly half of the English sailors had died of disease or starvation, though none of the ships was lost.

8

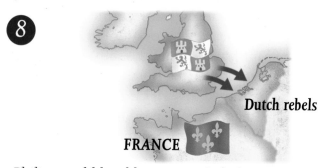

Philip would be able to use a Catholic England as a base against the Protestant Dutch rebels in the Netherlands.

Terrible weather wrecked many of the Spanish ships off the coasts of Scotland and Ireland. Local people looted any wrecks on shore. By September, only half the Spanish fleet had returned to Spain. Over 17,000 Spaniards had died. The English claimed victory. They issued a medal saying "God blew and they were scattered". Philip blamed the weather.

1 *Write a letter to King Philip, as if you were writing just after the defeat of the Armada. Explain carefully why you think the plan went wrong, and how he might be successful if he attacked again.*

A Spanish view of the Armada

Events in history are often described in different ways by different people or countries, depending on their point of view. A cartoon book about Philip II was published at the request of the Spanish Government in 1999. It was written to celebrate the 400th anniversary of Philip's death in 1598. This part tells the story of the Armada and has been translated into English.

1   Already damaged, the Armada anchored off Calais. It asked for help from the Duke of Parma but he could not give it.

2   Meanwhile, Drake stayed at anchor, waiting for the right moment to attack. One night, he launched eight badly damaged ships towards the Armada. They were set on fire. It came as a complete surprise.

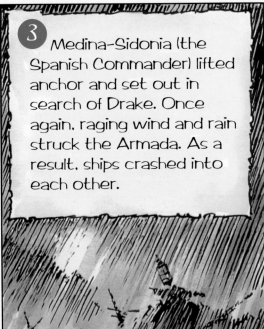

3   Medina-Sidonia (the Spanish Commander) lifted anchor and set out in search of Drake. Once again, raging wind and rain struck the Armada. As a result, ships crashed into each other.

... A Spanish view of the Armada

4 The smaller ships began to break up, forcing others into the coast of the Spanish Netherlands. Other ships were dragged into the North Sea.

5 The following morning, the English were there again. Medina-Sidonia and some of his commanders managed to gather together around 40 ships to confront Howard and Drake.

6 Once more the storm returned and scattered the Spanish fleet. Losses were high among the heavy Spanish ships.

7 Some of them were washed up in Holland, where the Dutch rebels captured them. Dutch ships joined the English to pursue what was left of the Armada.

Medina-Sidonia ordered the [su]rviving ships to sail [ar]ound the North of [S]cotland and return to [Sp]ain, passing Ireland on [th]e way. It was a long [an]d difficult journey [wi]th many deaths.

9 The remains of lifeless bodies and wrecked ships appeared everywhere.

10 Medina-Sidonia managed to reach Santander in September 1588. Little by little, some 60 ships returned. The rest had been lost for nothing.

1 The account of the failure of the Armada on pages 28–30 is a modern English version. The Spanish cartoon tells the same story from the arrival of the Armada off Calais. You will now compare the two stories.

Look at these statements. Each one gives a possible reason for the failure of the Armada. Give each statement a mark out of 5, where:

1 = not at all important ⟶ **5** = very important

Do this first from the view of the English account, and then from the view of the Spanish account.

The Duke of Parma was not ready when the Armada arrived off Calais.

The Spanish ships cut their anchors and panicked after the attack by English fire ships, breaking their formation.

Spanish cannons were badly made and poorly used.

The English badly damaged the Armada during the battle of Gravelines.

The Dutch rebels helped to defeat the Armada.

The bad weather helped to defeat the Armada.

2 How different are the two accounts? Can you suggest why this is?

3 Write a new set of captions to go with the Spanish cartoon, from an English point of view. You will need to write 10 captions.

Catholics or Puritans?

Who was the bigger threat to Elizabeth's Church of England?

Elizabeth I wanted to be different from her sister, Mary I. She didn't want to punish people for not going to the services of her Church of England. Yet if you didn't like her Church, you could also be seen as a threat to the Queen herself.

Catholics were one threat because they still believed the Pope was the real head of the Church. Puritans, the extreme Protestants, were also a threat because they didn't think the Church had changed enough, and was still too Catholic.

One way of trying to work out whether the Queen felt more threatened by Catholics or by Puritans, is to look at the different ways she treated them at different times during her reign.

1558–1576
How did the Queen treat Catholics?

◆ Punishments – fines for not going to Church of England services.

◆ In 1571, it became treason (a crime against the Queen herself) to say the Elizabeth had no right to be Queen or was a heretic.

Executions: 0

1558–1576
How did the Queen treat Puritans?

◆ Punishments – fines for not going to Church of England services.

◆ In 1566, 30 priests lost their jobs for refusing to wear **vestments** [special robes].

Executions: 0

1576–1585
How did the Queen treat Catholics?

◆ Punishments – fines were increased.

◆ Anybody taking part in a Catholic service could be put in prison for a year.

◆ In 1585 Catholic priests were given 40 days to leave England or face death. Some Catholics were found guilty of treason. For example one priest, Edmund Campion, was tortured and executed on false charges.

Executions: about 35 including 27 priests.

1576–1585
How did the Queen treat Puritans?

◆ Punishments – same as before. 200 priests lost their jobs for holding meetings banned by the Archbishop of Canterbury.

◆ John Stubbs had his hand cut off for writing a pamphlet criticising the Queen's possible marriage to a French, Catholic prince.

◆ Puritan leaders were sometimes imprisoned.

Executions: 0

What else was happening between **1576** and **1585**?

◆ Frequent Catholic plots to make Mary Queen of Scots become Queen of England.

◆ Tension mounted between Protestant England and Catholic Spain. Elizabeth backed raids on Spanish treasure ships and helped Dutch Protestant rebels against Philip II.

◆ The Pope sent a new wave of Catholic priests to England, called the Jesuits. They converted some Protestants.

1585–1603 **How did the Queen treat Catholics?**
◆ Punishments – same as before.
Executions: about 125, including Mary Queen of Scots (1587) and 74 priests.

1585–1603 **How did the Queen treat Puritans?**
◆ Punishments – same as before. Puritan leaders were sometimes imprisoned.
Executions: at least 2

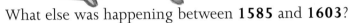

What else was happening between **1585** and **1603**?

◆ Full-scale war broke out between Protestant England and Catholic Spain. Any Catholics in England could then be seen as enemies of Elizabeth and allies of Spain.

◆ Some Puritans were attacking the bishops of the Church of England, and setting up separate places of worship. This was a threat to the Queen's authority over the Church, and the Church's control of the people.

◆ Mary Queen of Scots was executed.

◆ The Armada failed.

◆ The war with Spain lasted until 1604.

1 Copy this living graph.

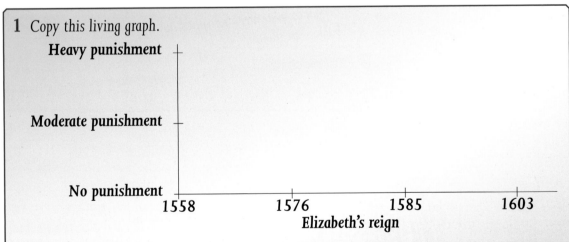

From the figures in the boxes, plot two lines onto the graph. Use **red** for Catholics and **blue** for Puritans.

2 Compare your graph with someone else's. How far do you agree or disagree? Why do you think that is?

3 On balance, who suffered more throughout Elizabeth's reign, Catholics or Puritans? Explain the reason for your answer.

In Britain today, most people live in towns and cities. They visit the countryside for its green beauty. In Elizabeth's time, life in the countryside was no picnic. Harvests could be bad and food was often expensive. Jobs were scarce, prices were rising and more and more people were being born, who then needed feeding. Poor people and beggars were everywhere. In the end, Elizabeth introduced a new law to control them.

How would these beggars be treated under the new law?

John

The Poor Law, 1601

- All begging was banned.
- Poor people with no work had to go back and live where they were born.
- Richer people paid a local tax to their parish, to help the "deserving poor".

The "deserving poor" (who deserved help) were:
- unemployed people, who were given work
- the old, the blind, and other poor not able to work
- the children of some poor people, who stayed with local craftsmen and learned a trade.

The "undeserving poor" (who did not deserve help) were:
- unemployed people who refused to work (they were sent to prison)
- beggars, who were whipped out of parishes until their backs "be bloody".

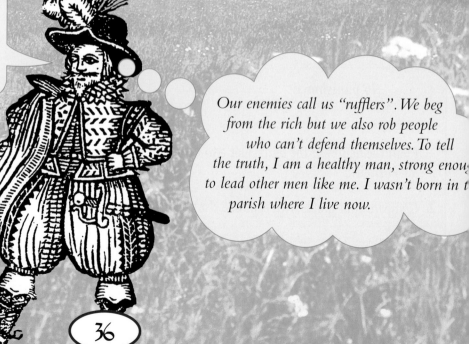

I lead a group of ex-soldiers who wander the country. I fought for the Queen against Spain. Now, I can't find work I want to do. Other people call men like us beggars, but we deserve some respect. After all, I was born here.

Our enemies call us "rufflers". We beg from the rich but we also rob people who can't defend themselves. To tell the truth, I am a healthy man, strong enou[g] to lead other men like me. I wasn't born in t[he] parish where I live now.

Tom

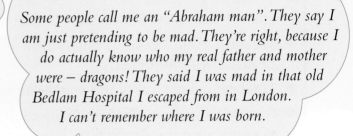

I'm Tom O'Bedlam. My father was the man in the moon and my mother a spirit of the air. I eat frogspawn from the pond.

Some people call me an "Abraham man". They say I am just pretending to be mad. They're right, because I do actually know who my real father and mother were – dragons! They said I was mad in that old Bedlam Hospital I escaped from in London. I can't remember where I was born.

Peter

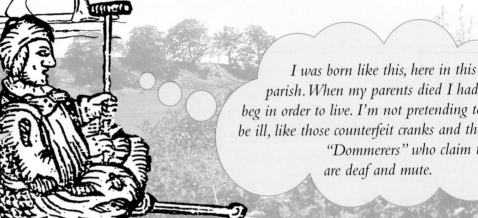

I am a cripple. I have to live from begging because I can't work. Can't you see my wooden leg and crutch?

I was born like this, here in this parish. When my parents died I had to beg in order to live. I'm not pretending to be ill, like those counterfeit cranks and those "Dommerers" who claim they are deaf and mute.

1 You are the overseer of the poor in a country parish. Your job is to report to the church wardens of the parish, who collect the local tax to pay for the new law. Which of the three people on these pages do you think is "deserving poor"? Who do you think is "undeserving poor"? Why?

2 Write a report like the one on the right to recommend what should be done about each of these three beggars.

REQUEST FOR FINANCIAL SUPPORT

Name _____ *Occupation* _____

Born locally yes / no / don't know

Financial condition _____

When did he last work? _____

Why does he not have work now? _____

Overseer's recommendation:
   deserving poor / undeserving poor

because _____

I recommend that he _____

Signed _____
OVERSEER OF THE POOR

37

1 Marriage

◆ Elizabeth would not marry a foreigner and risk letting another country control her.

◆ Elizabeth would not let an Englishman or his family control her.

◆ Elizabeth did not marry and provide an heir.

◆ As a single woman, Elizabeth partly controlled powerful men at court by flirting with them.

◆ If Elizabeth had died before 1603 (by which time she had agreed that James VI of Scotland would succeed her), there might have been a civil war between rivals for the throne. Since she had no children, there was no natural heir.

2 Religion

◆ Elizabeth's Church of England failed to attract both Catholics and Puritans.

◆ Elizabeth sometimes punished Puritan leaders.

◆ Elizabeth ordered the torture and execution of Catholics who plotted against her, and of some innocent Catholics.

◆ Elizabeth kept Catholics and Puritans under control.

◆ By 1603 Elizabeth's Church of England was strong and stable.

3 Mary Queen of Scots

◆ Elizabeth dithered for 19 years about Mary, encouraging Catholic plots.

◆ Elizabeth tried to control Mary by keeping her in prison for 19 years.

◆ Elizabeth ordered the killing of her own cousin and fellow Queen.

◆ Elizabeth ended a major threat to herself by executing an important Catholic rival.

4 Philip of Spain

◆ Elizabeth provoked the war with Spain by helping Dutch rebels and raiding Spanish treasure ships. She turned an old ally into a new enemy.

◆ Elizabeth's navy defeated the Armada in 1588. That gave England more power at sea.

◆ Elizabeth was lucky that bad weather defeated the Armada and that Philip's planning was so poor.

◆ Elizabeth curbed Philip's power by helping the Dutch rebels win their independence from Spain.

◆ The war with Spain went badly between 1589 and 1603.

◆ The war with Spain left England with huge debts.

◆ Spain was stopped from conquering England.

5 Poor people and beggars

◆ Elizabeth failed to stop the numbers of poor people and beggars growing.

◆ Elizabeth introduced the Poor Law in 1601. It was so successful it lasted 250 years.

◆ Elizabeth failed to stop prices rising.

◆ Elizabeth did not know enough about <u>why</u> there were so many poor people and beggars – for example, about the rise in numbers of babies being born.

6 Other problems

◆ Ireland was strictly controlled by the English.

◆ England was crippled by debts.

◆ Elizabeth appointed several Archbishops of Canterbury during her reign – but often delayed doing so in order to get money from their lands.

1 Look at each list of points about Elizabeth's problems. In each list, decide which points you think prove she was successful and list them in one colour. Then, with a different colour, list the points you think prove she was unsuccessful.

2 Discuss what you think the terms 'successful' and 'unsuccessful' mean. For example, does defeating the Armada count as being successful, or would you also expect Elizabeth to be winning the rest of the war with Spain?

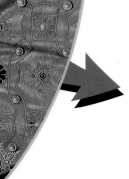

... How successfully did Elizabeth tackle the problems of her reign?

Deciding how successful Elizabeth was overall, is not easy. In many ways, just staying in power for so long counted as success – she was Queen for 45 years.

For each of her problems, there are at least two different ways of judging success.

Problem 1: Marriage

Does success mean …

| Marrying to provide an heir? | Controlling the country herself, by not marrying? |

Problem 2: Religion

Does success mean …

| Uniting all the people in one church? | Controlling the Church of England and both Catholics and Puritans? |

Problem 3: Mary Queen of Scots

Does success mean …

| Keeping Mary under control for 19 years? | Getting rid of a Catholic rival by killing her? |

Problem 4: Philip of Spain

Does success mean …

| Defending England against Spain? | Totally defeating Spain? |

Problem 5: Poor people and beggars

Does success mean …

| Making the people so rich that no-one is poor or needs to beg? | Starting to tackle the problem with a new Poor Law? |

What do you think?

1 Once you have decided what being successful means for each problem, you will be able to answer the question: How successfully did Elizabeth l tackle the problems of her reign? Use this writing frame and earlier pages in this section to help you with your answer.

In this essay I am going to explain how successfully Elizabeth tackled the problems of her reign.

Problem 1: Marriage

For this problem I think success means that _____

So Elizabeth was successful because _____

On the other hand, she was unsuccessful because _____

Who were the Stuarts?

Because Elizabeth I refused to marry, and had no children, her death in 1603 meant that there would be no more Tudor kings or queens. Instead, the crown of England and Ireland went to King James VI of Scotland. He became King James I of England and Ireland, and was the first of the Stuart kings. This brought England and Scotland together, after centuries of conflict.

married

Mary Queen of Scots
Born 1542
Queen of Scotland 1542–1587

This Catholic queen of Scotland was imprisoned and executed by her cousin, Elizabeth I, in 1587.

Henry Stewart, Lord Darnley
Born 1545, died 1567

Darnley was an attractive but vain and foolish man. Mary probably married him for his looks. He was murdered, possibly with Mary's help.

James Stuart
Born 1566
King James VI of Scotland
1567–1625
King James I of England and Ireland
1603–1625

James was a Protestant. His relationship with the English Parliament grew more and more difficult through his reign. He spent huge amounts of money, at court and then fighting wars. Parliament resented being asked for more and more money.

Charles Stuart
Born 1600
King of England, Scotland and Ireland 1625–1649

Would Charles's relationship with Parliament be any better than his father's had been?

This section of the book is about King Charles I, who ruled from 1625–1649, and his enemies.

The left-hand side of this page shows a painting of Charles from his lifetime. The other side shows a photograph of Sir Alec Guinness playing the role of Charles in a 1970 film. The film shows that Charles's reputation, and the events that happened during his reign, are still considered important nearly 400 years later.

What did successful rulers do?

Today, our kings and queens have no real power. Every important decision is made by Parliament. In the 17th century, a king or queen had enormous power. But using and keeping that power was really difficult. Remember how not even a clever ruler like Elizabeth could do just as she liked. She had to command respect and carefully keep control of the country. To do this, she sometimes made clever compromises — for example, her Church of England tried to keep both Catholics and Puritans happy.

This diagram shows the kind of things a 17th century ruler had to do in order to be successful.

Make clever compromises

Win wars

Keep control

Encourage trade

Produce an heir

Balance the books

What did successful rulers do?

Be brave

Work hard

Command respect

Stay alive and healthy

1 Think back to the decisions you made about how successful Elizabeth I was. Then list the things that a successful 17th century ruler did, in what you think is their order of importance.

How successful would King Charles I be? What did he do?

Meet the King

It is August 1642. Enemies of King Charles hold Scotland. Ireland is in chaos. England is on the verge of civil war. The King raises his standard [personal flag] at Nottingham, hoping to attract men to his army. Wars that will rage for nine years across three kingdoms are about to begin.

What if the King had been able to give a television interview? What might he have said? How had all this come about?

Interviewer: Good evening, your Majesty. Could you please tell us first where you believe your power comes from?

Charles: Well, my father was King James VI of Scotland. When his cousin Queen Elizabeth died in 1603, he also became King James I of England and Ireland. Then, when he died, I became King of Scotland, England and Ireland. We were all chosen to be ruler by God – that's called The Divine Right of Kings.

Interviewer: And what is your home life like, Sire?

Charles: I am very happily married. My wife, Queen Henrietta Maria, is French. As a Catholic, she worships in her own chapel and not in the buildings of my own Church of England. We have a happy family of fine children. I'm quite a shy person and I often stutter, especially in public. I live quite simply – for example I never eat or drink too much – but I like to surround myself with beautiful pictures and statues. It's very important for me to impress people and look the part of a king. My court painter, Anthony Van Dyck, paints me taller than I really am – I'm actually only five feet two inches.

Interviewer: What are your views on how the Church should be run, Sire?

Charles: As you know, I am head of the Church of England. I expect my bishops to make sure every church building is kept as it should be, with a rail around the altar and candles on top of it. Every priest should wear a **surplice** [a special shirt] and follow the services in the Book of Common Prayer. So far my Archbishop of Canterbury, William Laud, has done an excellent job in forcing the Church to be organised in this way.

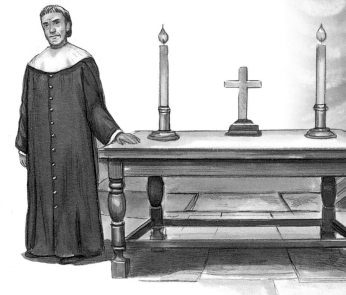

Interviewer: Does everyone agree with this?

Charles: No. Some of the people, the religious extremists who call themselves Puritans, disagree a lot. They don't like bishops, candles, surplices, or the Book of Common Prayer. They say I'm trying to turn the Church Catholic, and they call Laud a **papist** [an unkind word for a Catholic]. They say that the Queen, who's Catholic, has too much power. But I am not a papist. I don't obey the Pope in Rome, and Catholics in my kingdom pay fines for not going to official church services. The Puritans are <u>very</u> wrong. They want to seize power over the Church for themselves. They just don't like order.

The House of Commons

Interviewer: I see. And how does your Majesty get on with Parliament?

Charles: Not well, I have to say. Parliaments are a real nuisance. As you know, Parliament is split up into two Houses – the House of Lords, which includes my bishops and lords, and the House of Commons. The people in the House of Commons are rich men called Members of Parliament (MPs), who are elected by other rich men like themselves. Parliament's job is to pass laws, and I'm supposed to ask the House of Commons if I want to collect extra taxes. But it's the King who rules the country, not Parliament!

Interviewer: We're going to take a break now. Join us again in Part Two.

Meet the King Part Two

Interviewer: Welcome back, King Charles. You were telling us how you get on with Parliament …

Charles: Well, it's all come to a head now, as you know. I quarrelled with Parliament really badly in 1629 and actually ruled without them for 11 years. The real problems started in 1637, when I decided that the Scottish Church should have its own prayer book like the Church of England. It would make the Scottish Church more ordered, you see. But the Scots rebelled and I had to recall the English Parliament because I ran out of money to use against the Scots. The MPs in the Commons, especially the Puritans, then accused me of all sorts of things:

- ruling without Parliament for 11 years
- collecting what they said were illegal taxes, like the Ship Money to pay for the navy
- imposing order on the Church of England
- using force to get loans of money from rich people
- and using special law courts like the Star Chamber to force my wishes on the country.

Interviewer: So what did you do?

Charles: Well, at first I had to give Parliament some of what it wanted. I had to agree to:
- stop collecting taxes without Parliament's permission
- call a Parliament at least every three years
- put Archbishop Laud in prison
- stop using force
- get rid of special courts like the Star chamber
- execute my best and most loyal adviser, Lord Strafford.

Ship money was a tax which was only supposed to be paid when the navy needed more ships. Charles made it a regular tax.

If only I hadn't agreed to the death of Lord Strafford. He was a real friend.

46

Interviewer: Why did you give way to Parliament so much?

Charles: I couldn't really do anything else, because in the end only Parliament could let me collect enough taxes to run the country. The Scots controlled part of the north of England and my enemies in Parliament were in contact with them. If only I hadn't agreed to the death of Lord Strafford. He was a real friend.

Then last year, in 1641, there was a rebellion in Ireland and rumours reached England that thousands of Protestants had been massacred by Catholics. I wanted Parliament to pay for an army so that I could restore order in Ireland, but then Parliament demanded the right to control the soldiers. Of course, I refused this point blank and later took hundreds of armed men to the House of Commons to arrest five of my main enemies. Unfortunately, they were warned beforehand and managed to escape.

Now London is no longer safe for my family and supporters. That's why I've raised my standard here in Nottingham, to defend my rights and the rights of my subjects against the rebels and Puritans in Parliament. I ask all Englishmen who love their sovereign, their Church and their freedom under the rule of law to join me, in God's name.

The 350th anniversary of the raising of the Royal Standard in Nottingham

1 Look back at the success diagram for a ruler on page 43, and at how you ordered the things successful rulers had to do. Then look back through the interview with Charles I. Give him a mark out of ten for each of the ten things on page 43. (You may not be able to give him a mark for all of them.)

2 Use this successometer to decide how successful overall Charles I was as a ruler between 1629 and 1642.

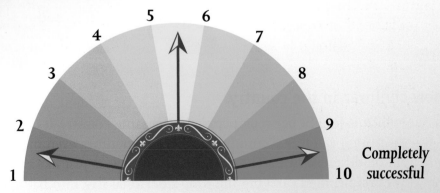

Unsuccessful 1 · · · 10 Completely successful

The King and Parliament were supposed to work together, each with their own job to do.

The King

God made me King.
I run the government.
I make peace and war.
Taxes are for me to spend.
I agree to new laws.
I control the soldiers and sailors.
I call Parliament when I want.
All the rich people support me.

Parliament

The House of Lords **The House of Commons**

We are all the bishops and the Lords of England and Wales. We help make new laws.

We are the Members of Parliament (MPs). We are ordinary men, with no title, though we are all fairly rich. Other rich men choose us to be MPs. We help make new laws. Only we can agree to new taxes for the King.

In 1642, when the King left London for Nottingham, the system of government broke down. The King and Parliament disagreed about:

How much power the King should have

How the Church of England should be run

Collecting taxes

Control of soldiers and sailors

How much power Parliament should have

There was now civil war in the country.

A **civil war** is one which is fought between people in the same country. It can be the worst type of war, because it can tear communities apart. Sometimes even members of the same family fight on different sides. The English Civil War was just like that. Sir Edmund Verney, for example, died carrying the King's personal flag into battle in 1642. His son supported Parliament.

Not all the rich people supported the King, and not all the MPs supported Parliament. Many people supported the side which they thought was more likely to win. Half of the MPs in the House of Commons sided with the King, and one third of the Lords sided with Parliament.

On the King's side

- The King's supporters were called Royalists.
- Their enemies nicknamed them 'Cavaliers', a word for wild Spanish horsemen.

Scottish Government

- From 1603 Scotland shared the same king with England, Wales and Ireland.
- In 1637, the Scots rebelled to stop Charles I interfering with the Scottish Church. They set up a **Scottish Government** to run Scotland the way <u>they</u> wanted.

On Parliament's side

- Parliament's supporters were called Parliamentarians.
- The Royalists nicknamed them 'Roundheads'.

Cavalier is meant to be an insult. It makes me sound foreign and Catholic. But I'm proud to be a Cavalier! It means I'm brave and loyal to my King.

You Roundhead!

You Cavalier!

Roundhead is supposed to poke fun at my short Puritan haircut. But I'm proud to be a Roundhead. I'm honest and brave, a true Protestant, fighting for God.

The New Model Army

- The New Model Army was formed in 1645 to fight on the side of Parliament.
- Discipline and organisation were very strong.
- The soldiers were known as 'Ironsides'.
- They believed very strongly that God was on their side.

Oliver Cromwell

- Oliver Cromwell was a Puritan MP.
- During the Civil War, he helped found the New Model Army and became its leader.
- He was a very religious man who became a brilliant soldier.

The ordinary people

- Many ordinary people did not want to fight at all, but were often forced to.
- They sometimes had to take soldiers into their homes and to feed them.
- Sometimes their homes and their churches were looted by soldiers from either side.

Between 1642 and 1648, two civil wars were fought between King Charles I and Parliament. The maps on this page and the next two pages show how support was divided between the two sides in 1642, 1646 and 1648. The larger the human figures, the more support and power they had. You are going to use these maps to help you answer the question: Were the King's enemies bound to fall out?

1642: Let battle commence!

Who is going to win in England? Whose side should we be on?

SCOTTISH GOVERNMENT

Edinburgh

I control half of England and Wales. My armies are better organised than Parliament's. I am confident I will win.

areas controlled by the King

areas controlled by Parliament

We control half of England and Wales but we are worried we may lose. We will have to re-organise our army. Maybe our Scottish friends will help us against the King.

Nottingham

KING

London

PARLIAMENT, House of Lords, House of Commons

1646: Defeat of the King

By 1646, the picture was very different. After four terrible years of war, the King had been defeated. The two most important battles were at Naseby and Marston Moor. Charles had finally surrendered to the Scottish Government's army at Newark, and was now a powerless prisoner.

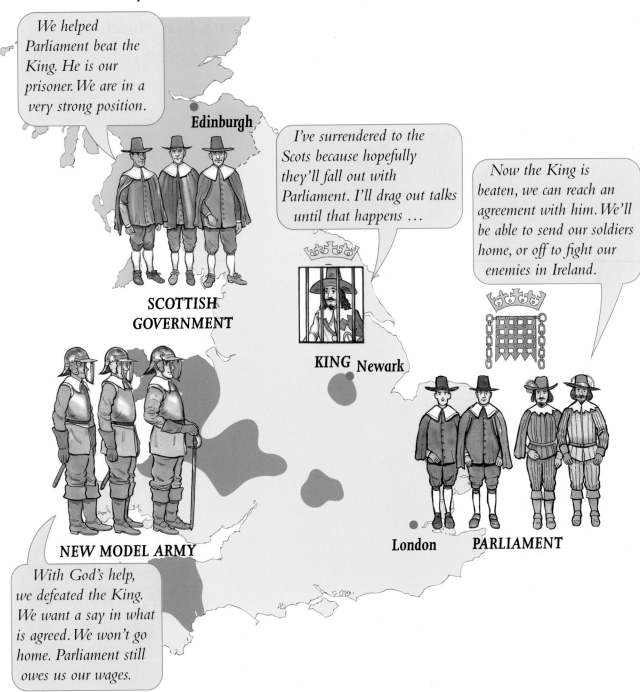

We helped Parliament beat the King. He is our prisoner. We are in a very strong position.

Edinburgh

I've surrendered to the Scots because hopefully they'll fall out with Parliament. I'll drag out talks until that happens …

Now the King is beaten, we can reach an agreement with him. We'll be able to send our soldiers home, or off to fight our enemies in Ireland.

SCOTTISH GOVERNMENT

KING Newark

NEW MODEL ARMY

With God's help, we defeated the King. We want a say in what is agreed. We won't go home. Parliament still owes us our wages.

London **PARLIAMENT**

The MPs of the House of Commons were becoming more important than the House of Lords. Parliament's New Model Army also had a will of its own. Its soldiers had beaten the King in God's name. They would not be happy with a back seat. Parliament, the Scottish Government and the New Model Army now waited to negotiate an agreement with Charles.

1648: The King's enemies begin to quarrel

By 1648, a second phase of the Civil War had changed things again.
The King had delayed negotiations with Parliament, hoping it would fall
out with the New Model Army. Then he made a separate agreement with
the Scottish Government. His supporters rose up against Parliament, and
a Scottish army invaded to help them – but Parliament's New Model
Army continued to win its battles, defeating the Scots at Preston.
The soldiers were in no mood for compromise …

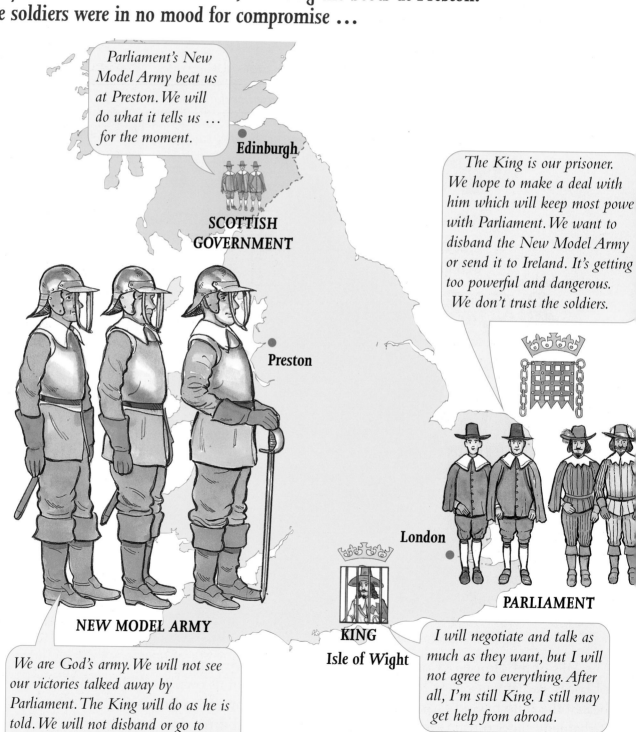

Parliament's New Model Army beat us at Preston. We will do what it tells us … for the moment.

Edinburgh

SCOTTISH GOVERNMENT

The King is our prisoner. We hope to make a deal with him which will keep most powe with Parliament. We want to disband the New Model Army or send it to Ireland. It's getting too powerful and dangerous. We don't trust the soldiers.

Preston

London

PARLIAMENT

NEW MODEL ARMY

KING
Isle of Wight

We are God's army. We will not see our victories talked away by Parliament. The King will do as he is told. We will not disband or go to Ireland. WHERE IS OUR PAY?

I will negotiate and talk as much as they want, but I will not agree to everything. After all, I'm still King. I still may get help from abroad.

Were the King's enemies **bound** to fall out? After all, in 1646 the New Model Army, Parliament and the Scottish Government had all been on the same side.

---

1 Look back at the map in **1642**. The diagram below shows how friendly or hostile the Scottish Government and the King were towards Parliament at the time.

very hostile	quite hostile	quite friendly	very friendly
✗		✗	
King		Scottish Government	

2 Look back at the map in **1646**. Draw a diagram like the one above and mark on it how friendly or hostile the Scottish Government, the King and the New Model Army were towards Parliament by 1646.

Were the Scottish Government and the New Model Army friendly or hostile towards each other? How likely were the King's enemies to fall out in 1646?

3 Now look back at the map in **1648** and draw another diagram to show how friendly or hostile the Scottish Government, the King and the New Model Army were towards Parliament by 1648. (Remember that the New Model Army was supposed to **obey** Parliament.)

How likely were the King's enemies to fall out in 1648? More likely than in 1646? If so, why? Were the King's enemies **bound** to fall out?

Why did the soldiers break ranks?

The soldiers of the New Model Army were angry and impatient. They had fought long and hard against the King. The blood of their comrades stained the battlefields of England. They believed God had shown He was on their side with victory after victory. They had protected Parliament and the freedoms of the people.

But what did they get in return? They were very unpopular in the country – most ordinary people didn't agree with what the soldiers believed in, and hated paying taxes for them. They were owed a lot of their pay, and Parliament was turning against them. Parliament also wanted to force everyone to worship in the buildings of the Church of England again. Yet most soldiers agreed that all Christians should be able to worship wherever and however they wanted.

It was to win this **tolerance** that so many had died. So when news reached the soldiers that the King would not agree with the Army's demands, they had to decide what to do.

How united was the New Model Army?

The New Model Army had fought against the King to protect Parliament. Now the King was defeated, yet still Parliament continued to try and reach an agreement with him even though he rejected the Army's ideas for the country. How much patience did the Army have left? And how united were the soldiers themselves?

Opinions differed about what to do, especially between the **officers** and the ordinary **soldiers**.

What should happen to the King?

We officers think that God is now against Charles Stuart. Parliament should put him on trial. Some of us want to make one of his sons king instead, or choose our own king. Perhaps we could even get rid of a king altogether.

*We agree about Charles Stuart. He is a **man of blood** and should be put on trial. But we think the country would be better without any king. Only Jesus should be our king! Let's have a **Commonwealth** instead.*

man of blood = guilty man
Commonwealth = a republic, a government with no king

What should happen to Parliament and to our wages?

This Parliament will not give us the wages we are owed. Let's close it down by force and give power to the MPs who are our friends. <u>They</u> will pay us.

Yes, but some of us want a new sort of Parliament, where more ordinary men get the vote as well.

What should happen to the Church of England?

Some of us think we should get rid of the Church of England. Protestants should be able to worship as they like. Some of us think we should still keep the Church of England though.

But why stop there? Some of us think that …

- people should be free to say and write what they think about all sorts of things
- everybody should be equal, with no so-called important people like lawyers to decide what we should do
- poor people should be able to live together on common land, sharing everything
- local people should be able to elect who rules over them.

1649: Who held power now?

The Army actually decided what to do very quickly. Colonel Pride took a troop of soldiers to Parliament and only allowed into the House of Commons those MPs who agreed with the Army's ideas. These MPs agreed to put the King on trial and planned to set up a Commonwealth. They also promised to do something about the soldiers' pay. Behind the scenes, the Army officers now held power.

The new Parliament carried out the plan, and **the King was sentenced to death**. The MPs then got rid of the House of Lords and set up a Commonwealth. Now, there was **no King**, **no bishops** and **no House of Lords**. Only the MPs in the House of Commons could decide how to rule the country. Backing them, were the soldiers of the New Model Army.

The trial of King Charles I

1 Look again at the argument opposite between the officer and the soldier. Whose ideas had become more important?

2 The ideas in the last speech bubble were very extreme at the time, and shocked a lot of people. Some of the ideas did not last, but some of them are considered 'normal' today. Which ones do we now accept?

On 30 January 1649, King Charles I was beheaded, on Parliament's orders. In 1971, the film **Cromwell** told the story like this.

1 Charles wears a hat and cloak and carries a prayer book. Charles's friend, Bishop Juxon, follows him.

The staircase is lined with silent Army officers and MPs.

2 There is a wooden block with ropes either side, tied to metal chains. Soldiers on horseback keep back the crowd.

The outside scaffold is coloured black.

3 Charles hands his hat and prayer book to Bishop Juxon.

4 The headsmen wear black masks

Charles says, "Well, gentlemen, are you afraid to kill your King with an open face?" (He stutters this in a Scottish accent.)

5 The crowd is silent.

I will not delay you long but say only this as God is my witness. I forgive those who brought me here and I pray that my death be not laid to their charge. For I do endeavour even to the last to maintain the peace of my kingdom. I go from a corruptible to an incorruptible crown.

6 After giving his cloak and ribbon to Juxon, Charles tucks his hair under a cap.

Will that suffice?

7 The axe severs the King's head with one blow.

It's supposed to be January, but the trees have green leaves!

Behold the head of a traitor!

8

The crowd is silent. Then a loud groaning spreads through the crowd.

In 1998, the historian Robert Partridge wrote a book about Charles I. What follows is a shortened version of his retelling of the story of Charles's death.

It was a cold day. The King, wearing a cloak and carrying a cane [stick], walked onto the black-covered scaffold with his friend Bishop Juxon. The block stood in the centre, with the axe lying nearby. The floor was sprinkled with sand to soak up blood. Four heavy iron staples were driven into the floor. Ropes were attached to the staples and littered the floor. If the King resisted, he would be dragged to the block using the ropes. There was also a cheap coffin.

The small platform was crowded, including two or three shorthand writers with notebooks and inkpots, ready to record the King's last words. The two headsmen wore masks as disguises, one with a hat and the other with a grey wig and beard.

The space between the scaffold and the rails was packed with soldiers, while beyond the rails soldiers on horseback mingled with the waiting crowds in the streets. The King made his speech from notes written on a small piece of paper he took from his pocket. His words could only be heard by the 15 or so people on the scaffold.

... Why do historians and film makers tell the same story differently?

This is part of the King's speech. The modern meaning is given under each line.

"Truly I desire their liberty and freedom as much as anybody whomsoever, but I must
I honestly want my people to be free as much as anybody else does, but I must

tell you their liberty and freedom consists in having of government, those laws by
tell you that the people's freedom lies in having a government which keeps laws

which their life and their goods may be most their own. It is not for having a share in
that allow the people to hold on to their own lives and belongings. Freedom is not about the people having a share in

government, Sir, that is nothing pertaining to them. A subject and a Sovereign are
government, Sir, that is nothing to do with them. A King and an ordinary person are

clear different things ... it was for this that now I am come here. If I would have given
quite different things ... that is the reason I am here. If I had given

way to an arbitrary power, for to have all laws changed to the power of the sword, I
in to force [the Army] and allowed all laws to be changed by force, I

needed not to have come here; and therefore I tell you (and I pray to God it be not
would not be here, and therefore I tell you (and I pray to God He does not

laid to your charge) that I am a martyr of the people."
blame you for my death) that I am dying to defend the people.

His speech ended, the King spoke to the two headsmen. There is no account of his actual words, but he explained that he would kneel with his head on the block and then make a sign for the blow to be struck. With the help of Bishop Juxon, he put on a cap and pushed his hair beneath it.

"There is but one stage more," said Juxon. Charles replied, "I go from a corruptible to an incorruptible crown [from a corrupt earthly kingdom to the incorrupt kingdom of heaven], where no disturbance can be, no disturbance in the world."

Charles stood for a moment, praying in silence. He then slipped off his cloak and lay his head on the block. With one blow, his head was severed from his body. One of the headsmen held the head up to the crowd, which set up a terrible groaning.

At public executions, it was usual for the head to be held up with the cry of "Behold the head of a traitor". An eyewitness account says specifically that the executioner was silent, and none of the other publications of the time disagrees with this.

1 You are now going to compare carefully the film and the historian's account. Write out and fill in this grid.

Question	Film	Account
1 What did the King wear?		
2 What season was it?		
3 What was on the scaffold?		
4 How much did the King say?		
5 How many people heard his speech?		
6 What did he say to the headsmen?		
7 What did the headsmen wear?		
8 What happened just after the King's head was severed?		

2 There are differences between the film and the historian's account. A historian should look at original sources and what other historians have said, so that what they write is as **accurate** as possible. However, historians have to **interpret** the evidence they find, sometimes using their imagination. They also usually have their own point of view. People who make historical films like *Cromwell* want their films to be successful and entertaining. They may do this by **adapting** events to make them more entertaining, rather than telling them accurately. *Cromwell* is meant to be accurate, but is it? Look at the following ways that film makers may try to increase the size of their audience. Can you find examples of each one in the *Cromwell* extract?

The film makers:

◆ changed the order in which events actually happened

◆ made the actors and actresses look more modern

◆ modernised the language to make it easier to understand, and changed what was actually said

◆ speeded up the action and cut out the boring details

◆ cut out much of the blood and violence, to make it more of a family film

3 More people will learn about events in the past if historical films are more popular. But how accurate are they? Look back at your answers to question 2. Did you find evidence that the film makers had included fact? If so, how much? In pairs, decide how close to the truth the death scene in *Cromwell* was. Explain your answer.

4 Write and design your own film scene of Charles I's death. How and why would yours be different from the *Cromwell* version?

Was Oliver Cromwell a 'war criminal'?

Since the end of the Second World War (1939–1945), special courts have been set up with judges from different countries. These courts have to decide if the prisoners before them are guilty of *war crimes*.

An ordinary criminal is someone who breaks the laws of a country. A **war criminal** is someone who breaks the rules of war. These rules include:

> 1. You must not deliberately kill enemy prisoners of war after they have surrendered.
> 2. You must not deliberately kill innocent civilians (ordinary people who don't fight).

Someone found guilty of breaking these rules would be a war criminal and would be imprisoned. (Until recently, they could also be executed.)

War crime trials still take place today. But are war crimes just a modern problem? Did people break the rules of war in the 17th century too?

Oliver Cromwell

Oliver Cromwell became one of the English Parliament's most successful leaders and generals. He ruled the Commonwealth of England, Scotland and Ireland as Lord Protector from 1653 until his death in 1658. He nearly became king. But what **kind** of soldier was he? Did he break the rules of war?

Over the next few pages you are going to investigate three charges against Cromwell which will help you answer the question: was Oliver Cromwell a 'war criminal'?

Oliver Cromwell deliberately ordered the execution of rebel soldiers from his own army after they had surrendered to him.

After the execution of the King in 1649, the English Parliament, supported by the Army, declared a Commonwealth. The new Commonwealth was threatened by royalists in Scotland and Ireland who might have invaded to set up Charles II (son of Charles I) as King. Parliament ordered Oliver Cromwell and his army to Ireland to defeat its enemies there. But many soldiers were very angry. They had not been paid for months and now they were expected to just go and fight again in Ireland. Many soldiers were also listening to groups of civilians who had extreme ideas (look at the box below for more information). The Levellers in particular posed a threat.

Soldiers in London, Banbury and Salisbury rebelled. They refused to fight in Ireland and demanded their back pay. Some openly supported the Levellers. On 10 May, thousands of rebel soldiers left Salisbury and marched on Burford. Cromwell moved his own soldiers swiftly, covering 50 miles a day on horseback. They surprised the rebels at night and most of them surrendered when they were promised a **pardon** [to be forgiven]. But Cromwell broke his promise. Four of the rebel leaders were put on trial and three were executed. The rebellion was over.

What did Levellers believe?

◆ The country should be ruled by a parliament elected once a year by all men.

◆ The Church of England should be **abolished** [got rid of].

◆ People should be able to worship however they liked (even Catholics).

What did Diggers believe?

◆ The rich should give up their private wealth and property, which should be totally banned.

◆ Poor people should be able to farm whatever land they wanted.

◆ The country should be ruled by officials elected once a year.

John Lilburne, leader of the Levellers, who was locked up in the Tower of London

1 Do you think Oliver Cromwell did the right thing?

2 Look back at the descriptions of war crimes on page 60. Do you think Cromwell was guilty of a war crime when the rebel leaders were killed at Burford? Make a list of the evidence you would use to prove your case.

... Was Oliver Cromwell a 'war criminal'?

WAR CRIME CHARGE TWO

Oliver Cromwell ordered the massacre of about 2,000 civilians and enemy soldiers, after they had surrendered, in the town of Drogheda, Ireland, on 11 September 1649.

Cromwell took his New Model Army soldiers to Drogheda, determined to crush the royalists and to get revenge for what they believed was the terrible massacre [mass killing] of Protestants by Irish Catholics in 1641. The town fell quickly. Even though Cromwell knew that many enemy soldiers had surrendered to his men, a massacre followed. Cromwell wrote ...

Ireland in 1649

I believe we put to the sword the whole number of defenders.

I think that night they put to the sword 2,000 men.

I ordered the steeple of St Peter's to be fired, when one of them was heard to say, "God damn me, God confound me, I burn, I burn."

I do not believe, neither do I hear, that any soldie[r] escaped with his life.

A school history book for Irish children, written in 1991, said:

> They were all cut down and no mercy was shown to man, woman or child for twenty-four hours. Not a dozen escaped out of Drogheda, townspeople or soldiers.

An Irish 19th century picture of the taking of Drogheda

1 Look back at the descriptions of war crimes on page 60. Do you think Oliver Cromwell was guilty of a war crime at Drogheda? Make a list of the evidence you would use to prove your case.

Oliver Cromwell ordered the massacre of about 3,000 citizens and enemy soldiers, after they surrendered, in the town of Wexford, Ireland on 11 October 1649.

Cromwell's army marched north from Drogheda to take the royalist town of Wexford. On 11 October, the governor of Wexford surrendered the town to Cromwell's men, who then turned the town's cannon on the defenders. The defenders fled in terror. Cromwell's soldiers poured over the walls. The fighting lasted for just one hour. Some of the townspeople fled by boat. Two boats overturned in the river, sending 300 people, including women and children, to a watery grave.

1 Look back at the descriptions of war crimes on page 60. Do you think Oliver Cromwell was guilty of a war crime at Wexford? Make a list of the evidence you would use to prove your case.

GUILTY ON ALL COUNTS?

On the surface, Cromwell looks guilty of all three charges. Who could defend such a war criminal? Each year at Burford some people, who see the rebel soldiers as Leveller heroes, pay tribute to the 'martyrs' Cromwell killed. His reputation in Ireland is even worse. But it is always worth looking at evidence more closely. Look back at page 61, then read the chart below carefully.

THE PROSECUTION: WAR CRIME CHARGE ONE	IN DEFENCE OF CROMWELL
Oliver Cromwell deliberately ordered the execution of rebel soldiers from his own army after they had surrendered to him.	The three rebel soldiers were not ordinary prisoners of war. They were not Cromwell's enemies in the same way that royalists or foreigners were. The soldiers came from his own army and it was up to him how he treated them. Therefore, punishing the rebels was not a war crime. In fact, Cromwell kept his promise to most of the rebel prisoners. They were forgiven. Only the three ringleaders died.

2 Do you still think Cromwell was guilty of a war crime at Burford? If you have changed your mind, why have you done so?

... Was Oliver Cromwell a war criminal?

This is Tom Reilly. Tom is an Irish historian who was born in Drogheda. He was brought up on tales of Cromwell's cruelty. But Tom wasn't happy about what he was told. He wanted to find out the *real* story of Cromwell's time in Ireland. This is what he found out about what Cromwell did at Drogheda.

Tom Reilly with Cromwell's death mask

A Rules of war in 1649 said that you must ask your enemies to surrender before you fought them. If they refused and fought, you could kill them even if they later chose to surrender. **Killing prisoners in 1649 was not always a war crime.**

B Lord Ormonde, the royalist commander in Ireland, **never accused Cromwell** of massacring unarmed civilians.

C Cromwell gave strict orders to his soldiers to kill their enemies at Drogheda, and **not to take prisoners.**

D No eyewitness accounts from 1649 (or just after) refer to the killing of unarmed civilians.

E Local records from Drogheda show that hundreds of people turned up for a regular meeting on 5 October 1649, only a month after the fighting. **No massacre was discussed.**

F Not all Drogheda's defenders **were killed by Cromwell's men.** Some prisoners were sent in chains to Barbados, to work in the fields there.

G There are **no records of mass burials** in Drogheda in 1649.

H Wild stories about massacres of unarmed civilians were spread **long after 1649** to make Cromwell look bad. Some Irish historians have repeated them to attack the English.

I Cromwell gave his soldiers strict instructions **not to harm unarmed civilians.**

Cromwell wrote a letter to the royalist governor of Drogheda on 10 September 1649, the day before the town fell. It says (in modern English):

" *Sir, I brought the army of the English Parliament to this town. The town must accept my authority. To stop bloodshed, I demand your surrender at once. If you refuse, you cannot blame me for what happens afterwards.*

O. Cromwell"

The governor refused to surrender.

This is what Tom Reilly found out about what Cromwell did at Wexford.

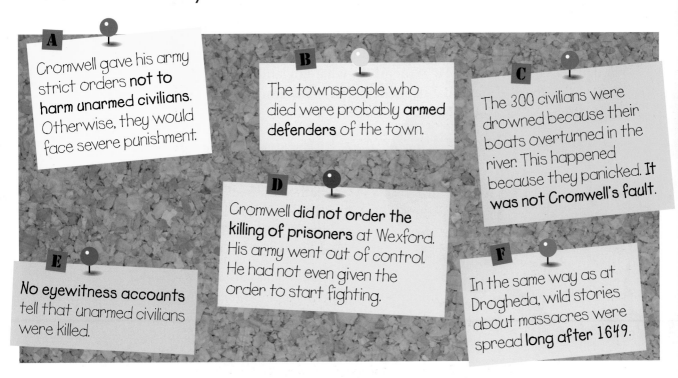

A Cromwell gave his army strict orders **not to harm unarmed civilians**. Otherwise, they would face severe punishment.

B The townspeople who died were probably **armed defenders** of the town.

C The 300 civilians were drowned because their boats overturned in the river. This happened because they panicked. It **was not Cromwell's fault**.

D Cromwell **did not order the killing of prisoners** at Wexford. His army went out of control. He had not even given the order to start fighting.

E **No eyewitness accounts** tell that unarmed civilians were killed.

F In the same way as at Drogheda, wild stories about massacres were spread **long after 1649**.

---

1 Look back at the chart on page 63 which defends Cromwell against *War Crime Charge One*. Then draw the chart below and fill in the blank column in your own words, to defend him against *Charge Two*. Use the information on the opposite page.

THE PROSECUTION: WAR CRIME CHARGE TWO	IN DEFENCE OF CROMWELL
Oliver Cromwell ordered the massacre of about 2,000 innocent civilians and enemy soldiers, after they had surrendered, in the town of Drogheda, Ireland on 11 September 1649.	

2 Now complete another chart for *War Crime Charge Three*. Use the information on these pages, and what you know about war crimes, to help you defend Cromwell.

3 Overall, do you agree or disagree that Oliver Cromwell was a war criminal? If you find it hard to choose and think you need more information, draw up a list of questions you would like to ask about his actions at Burford, Drogheda and Wexford, to help you decide.

What happened after Cromwell died?

It is 1673.

This is Old Jack. He was a soldier in the New Model Army, loyal to Cromwell. He was also a Puritan. He remembers what England was like under Oliver Cromwell – and what happened after his death.

The head of Oliver Cromwell

Those were the good old days. When Oliver was here, we were a strong Protestant country, with God on our side. We defeated everyone – royalists, Scots, Irish, Dutch, even the Spanish. Oliver was respected throughout Europe. It made you proud to be English.

You should have seen the funeral. They buried him like a king.

For weeks people came to see Cromwell's body lying in state.

James, Duke of York, the younger brother of King Charles II

No wonder God punished us by sending the Plague, and then that terrible fire in 1666, which destroyed a lot of London. He's judging this nation. None of this would have happened under Oliver. And to top it all, the King's younger brother James – who may well be our next king – has become a Catholic! Where will it all end?

Then everything began to fall apart. I suppose he did leave the country in a lot of debt because of all his wars. His son Richard took over at first, but he wasn't strong like his father. Then, in 1660, Parliament asked Charles I's son to come back. He was 'restored' to the throne as Charles II.

A king is restored. Charles II returns to London. The crowds adored him.

So now we have a king again. Those rotten royalists have dug up Oliver's body and stuck his head on a pole at Westminster. Godless cowards. He was a better man than any of them! And under this wicked King, London has become a den of vice! Like their King, men swear, gamble, drink and eat too much, go to the theatre, play sport on Sundays, and wear fancy clothes that make them look like women.

Then there are these terrible women. I've lost count of the King's mistresses! No wonder God has cursed him — he has lots of illegitimate children but the King and Queen have no children themselves, and no heir.

Three of Charles II's mistresses (from left): Louise de Keroualle, Nell Gwynne and Barbara Villiers

1 Read the memories of Old Jack. Why do you think people like him got so angry? What do you think a supporter of Charles II might say? For example, how would he remember Cromwell?

2 Think back over all the changes that Old Jack saw in his lifetime:
   ◆ the rule of Charles I
   ◆ the Commonwealth and Cromwell
   ◆ the Civil War
   ◆ the Restoration of Charles II
   ◆ the execution of a king
   ◆ the Great Plague and the Great Fire

Then look back at the events of Old Meg's life on pages 5–7. Do you think she saw as many changes as Old Jack did?

Charles II died in 1685. Although he had 13 children, none of them could take the throne because they were all illegitimate. Instead, his younger brother James became King. More upheaval would soon follow...

Who fought at the Battle of Culloden?

At 1.30 in the afternoon of 16th April 1746, Prince Charles Edward Stuart watched the front ranks of his Scottish Highland soldiers charge desperately towards their red-coated enemy on Culloden Moor. The Highlanders had stood their ground fiercely as they lost comrades right and left under terrible enemy fire. Some in the tightly-packed ranks had deliberately fallen to the ground to protect themselves. Others had fled in fear.

Rain and hail lashed against the Highlanders as they shouted their bloodcurdling battle cries and swept towards the enemy. Many times in the past, the redcoats had broken ranks in panic before the fierce Highland charge. Not this time.

The Highlanders became confused, caught in the thick smoke of enemy cannon. As it cleared, a line of redcoats, 30 metres away, levelled their guns and fired at the same time. Then that first rank knelt to re-load their guns, while the ranks behind fired over their heads.

The Highlanders who reached the enemy front line fought hand to hand, their swords against redcoat bayonets. Would Highland bravery be enough this time?

By 3 o'clock in the afternoon, the redcoat commander William, Duke of Cumberland, knew victory was his. His cavalry successfully attacked the Highlanders from behind their own lines. Prince Charles Edward Stuart fled the battlefield. His brave Highlanders tried to retreat as fast as they could. The redcoats advanced steadily through the heather, bayonetting the wounded and dying where they lay.

The Duke thanked his men, riding in front of the ranks of redcoats. As he passed, the men put their hats high on their bayonets and roared "Billy, Billy" in approval. The Duke was sometimes called "Sweet William" too, but in the next days and months, as his redcoats ruthlessly hunted down their Highland enemies, he gained a new nickname – "Butcher Cumberland".

To Prince Charles Edward Stuart, 16th April 1746 was a disaster; to the Duke of Cumberland, a God-given victory. But these two men were cousins…

Why were they fighting this battle in the first place?

What brought Prince Charles to Culloden?

What was at stake?

Look at the old smears of paint on this piece of wood. They hide a secret – a secret dangerous enough to threaten the life of the owner.

With a cylinder placed on the wood, the reflection reveals a secret painting. It is Charles Edward Stuart (sometimes called Bonnie Prince Charlie), leader of the Jacobites at the Battle of Culloden.

So great was the defeat at Culloden, that it was very dangerous afterwards to be caught with even a picture of Bonnie Prince Charlie. The Jacobites had to keep their beliefs hidden, just as this picture is hidden.

- ◆ The **Jacobites** were supporters of the Stuart family who claimed the crowns of England, Scotland and Ireland for themselves.

- ◆ James II was the last of the Stuarts to reign. He was overthrown in 1688.

- ◆ The name 'Jacobite' comes from the Latin word for James – Jacobus.

But how close to success did the Jacobites come? In this section of the book, you are going to investigate just how close the Jacobites came to winning back power.

The story really starts with James II of England and Ireland, who was called James VII in Scotland.

This is James II. He was a son of Charles I and became King in 1685 when his older brother Charles II died. Like his father, James believed in the **Divine Right of Kings** – that kings had a God-given right to rule. He was also Catholic, while England was now officially a Protestant country. All this meant trouble …

James wanted to:	English Protestants feared that:
◆ make life easier for fellow Catholics by getting rid of fines and laws against them	◆ James would turn England Catholic again, and reduce the power of the Church of England
◆ reduce Parliament's power and increase his own	◆ James would create an **absolute** government, where he would rule on his own without Parliament (like the King of France)
◆ create a powerful army with Catholic officers	◆ James would create a Catholic army which would enforce royal control

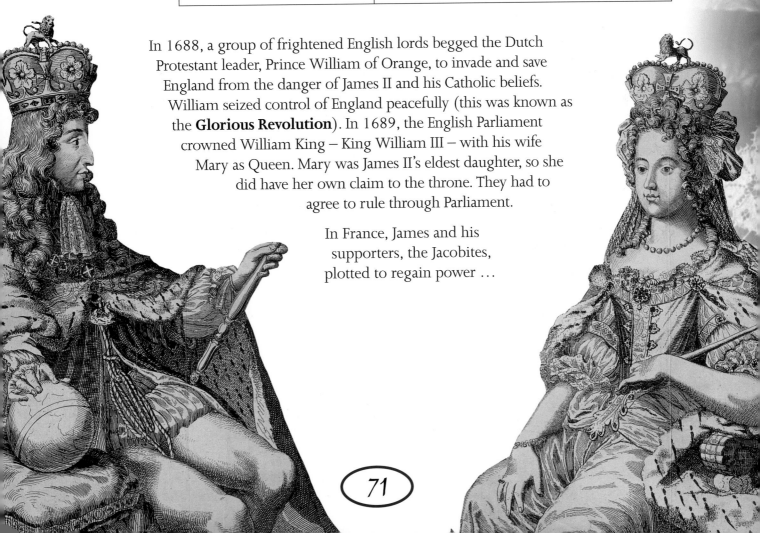

In 1688, a group of frightened English lords begged the Dutch Protestant leader, Prince William of Orange, to invade and save England from the danger of James II and his Catholic beliefs. William seized control of England peacefully (this was known as the **Glorious Revolution**). In 1689, the English Parliament crowned William King – King William III – with his wife Mary as Queen. Mary was James II's eldest daughter, so she did have her own claim to the throne. They had to agree to rule through Parliament.

In France, James and his supporters, the Jacobites, plotted to regain power …

71

After the overthrow of James II in 1688, his supporters were scattered across the three kingdoms of England, Scotland and Ireland – or else were with James in France. In order for the Jacobites to win back power, they needed a lot of things to work together in their favour ...

1 A strong army

The Jacobites needed a large army of experienced soldiers with plenty of weapons and ammunition.

2 Foreign help

The Jacobites needed money, men and weapons from powerful countries like France.

SUCCESS

3 Popular support

The Jacobites needed support from ordinary people in England, Scotland and Ireland. They needed men to volunteer for any armies they organised or that invaded from abroad.

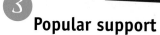

4 Good leadership

The Jacobites needed good leaders who could:

◆ inspire loyalty

◆ lead bravely

◆ make wise decisions quickly and effectively

◆ keep control of their soldiers.

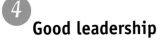

5 A weaker enemy

The Jacobites had more chance of success if their enemies were weak and disorganised.

6 Luck

The Jacobites could be helped by chance factors beyond their control, for example good weather allowing a foreign navy to land soldiers, or the death of an enemy leader.

---

1 In a pair, decide which of the factors on these pages might be the most important for the Jacobites in an attempt to win back power. Then add the other factors in order of importance. Discuss your ideas with another pair.

2 Imagine you are a secret Jacobite supporter. Write a letter to King James advising him on what he needs to do to win back power. Remember to be polite and formal – after all, he is your king!

Between 1689 and 1746, the Jacobites were to make four main attempts to win back power. How close to success would they come? Using factors 1–6 on these pages, you will decide how close they came to regaining power at each attempt.

Rebellion 1: Ireland 1689–1691

How close to success did the Jacobites come?

1 Although he lost power in England in 1688, James II still controlled most of Ireland:

Londonderry

Enniskillen

Dublin

- ◆ The Catholic Earl of Tyrconnell ruled Ireland in James's name, with the support of ordinary Catholics. Catholics were the majority of the people.

- ◆ Tyrconnell's army was trying to starve the Protestant cities of Londonderry and Enniskillen into surrender. The Protestants supported King William of England.

- ◆ Blessed with good weather, James II landed in Ireland in March 1689, with French money and officers, and weapons for 20,000 men.

We must free all of Ireland.

We must invade Scotland.

I don't know what to do.

2 The Jacobites in Ireland could not agree what to do:

- ◆ Tyrconnell was only interested in Ireland itself, not the total Jacobite cause.

- ◆ Some of James's advisers wanted to invade Scotland from Ireland.

- ◆ The French wanted to help spin out a long war in Ireland, because this would hurt their Protestant enemy, King William III of England.

- ◆ James was not sure what to do.

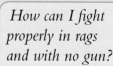

How can I fight properly in rags and with no gun?

3 The Jacobites mostly relied on Tyrconnell's army, <u>but</u>:

- ◆ Some of his soldiers were only dressed in rags, with no shoes.

- ◆ Only a few had guns.

- ◆ Money and food were very short.

In July 1689, the Jacobites had to give up trying to take Londonderry, and the Protestants of Enniskillen defeated them in battle.

4

In June 1690, King William of England himself arrived in Ireland.

◆ William was a good general.

◆ He had an army of 36,000 men, compared to James's army of 25,000.

William and James fought each other at the Battle of the Boyne on 1st July, 1690. A stray bullet <u>nearly</u> killed William, but he lived and defeated the Jacobites. James fled back to France. Within a year, the remaining Jacobites were defeated. Protestants took revenge on Irish Catholics for supporting James by taking away many of their lands and rights.

The Battle of the Boyne

1 Write out this diagram under the heading **Rebellion 1: Ireland 1689–1691**.

Write a sentence or paragraph for each factor to explain what happened in Ireland between 1689 and 1691. For example, under **Good leadership**, you might put:
James II and the Jacobites could not agree about what to do.
Leadership was poor.
(So this would not have helped them be successful.)

2 Now decide how close to success you think the Jacobites came. Use a scale of 1 – 10, like this:

1	2	3	4	5	6	7	8	9	10
Not close to success	Quite close to success	Very close to success							

Rebellion 2: Scotland 1689

How close to success did the Jacobites come?

Scotland was a country the Jacobites badly wanted to gain control of. Their support should naturally have come from Scotland, because the Stuarts were originally Scottish kings.

In 1689, Scotland was strongly divided between the Lowlands and the Highlands. Scots in the Lowlands were mostly Protestants. They disliked their King, James VII, who had already been overthrown in England (as King James II). Following England's example, the Protestant Scottish Government gave the crown to William and Mary of England instead.

Killiecrankie

Edinburgh

The Highlands were like a different country. Many people spoke Gaelic, a different language from the one spoken in the English-speaking Lowlands.

◆ They were organised into **clans** (groups of related families), who had to obey their family chief.

◆ Highlanders were fierce and wild fighters, often feuding amongst themselves.

◆ Some clans were still Catholic, and loyal to King James.

◆ Lowland Scots hated and despised Scots from the Highlands.

◆ Highlanders thought Scots from the Lowlands were soft and weak.

A Highland chief

In 1689, John Graham of Claverhouse, a Jacobite Lord from the Lowlands, organised an army to win back control of Scotland for James. He had no foreign help, and hardly any Lowlands Scots joined him. Instead, Claverhouse went to the Highlands and got more support there.

His army ambushed Government redcoats in a highland pass at Killiecrankie. The Government soldiers fled, leaving many dead and wounded behind them. However, although the ambush was successful, Claverhouse was killed. His army, left without a leader, disbanded.

John Graham (inset) and the pass at Killiecrankie

1 Write out this diagram under the heading **Rebellion 2: Scotland 1689**.

A strong army

Good leadership

Foreign help

SUCCESS

A weaker enemy

Luck

Popular support

Write a sentence or paragraph for each factor to explain what happened in Scotland in 1689. For example, under **Foreign help**, you might put:
John Graham of Claverhouse had no foreign support for his rebellion. This meant that …

2 Then use the same scale of 1–10 to decide how close to success the Jacobites came this time:

1	2	3	4	5	6	7	8	9	10
Not close to success				Quite close to success					Very close to success

By 1691, William III was in control of all of England, Scotland and Ireland. Jacobites still plotted for James's return, but would events help or hinder them? Would time weaken William's control and increase support for James? Read what happened next to find out.

William Patterso[n], founder of the Bank of England

1 The Bank of England 1694

In 1694, the English Parliament set up the Bank of England. It meant that wealthy English people could lend money to William's Government so that he always had enough money to continue his war against France. At one stroke, this solved the King's need for money.

Before, kings like Charles I usually had to rely on taxes from Parliament to keep going. James II had relied on money from his friend, the King of France. Now, as long as William ruled <u>with</u> the English Parliament, he could rely on taxes from them <u>and</u> loans from the Bank of England. There was little danger of running out of money.

Would this help or hinder the Jacobites? In what way?

2 The Act of Settlement 1700

In 1700, the English Parliament passed a law called the Act of Settlement. It gave Parliament new powers over the kings of England and Ireland. For example, no king or queen would be able to leave the country in future without Parliament's permission. This is still the law today.

The first entries in the Bank's accounts

The Act of Settlement also:

◆ Said that all kings and queens of England and Ireland <u>had</u> to be members of the Protestant Church of England.

◆ Banned Catholics like James II from ever being King.

◆ After William's death, gave the crown to James's second daughter, Anne (a Protestant).

◆ After Anne's death, gave the crown to a distant German cousin, Sophia, and then her son George (both Protestants).

◆ It ignored James Stuart, the Catholic son of James II, altogether.

◆ Paid off Scottish debts.

Would this help or hinder the Jacobites? In what way?

James II of England and Ireland
(James VII of Scotland)

Mary II **m.** William III   Anne   James   Sophia

✔   ✔   ✘   ✔

George

✔

✔ = Protestant

✘ = Catholic

English victories over France 1702–1711

James II died in Paris in 1701, but the King of France backed the claim of James's son to be King James III of England and Ireland (and James VIII of Scotland). In London, Anne became the actual Queen in 1702. For years, her armies struggled with those of King Louis XIV of France.

Her great commander, John Churchill, Duke of Marlborough, defeated French armies in many battles. His armies were partly paid for by Bank of England loans.

Would this help or hinder the Jacobites? In what way?

John Churchill, Duke of Marlborough

> **1** Write a short news report to explain the main events between 1691 and 1715, and whether they would help or hinder the Jacobites.

... 1691–1715: Would time help or hinder the Jacobites?

4 The Treaty of Union 1707

As England itself became a richer and more important country, Scotland fell behind. Although Scotland shared its king or queen with England and Ireland, it was still an independent kingdom with its own Parliament.

The Scots could still pass their own laws. Many Scots were **envious of English wealth** and at the same time **resented English power**. The English Parliament would not allow Scottish merchants to trade freely with English settlements in North America or elsewhere, and prevented Scots from starting settlements of their own abroad.

Under Queen Anne, relations between England and Scotland became really bad.

English politicians offered Scottish politicians a deal:

What the English offered	What the Scots stood to gain	What the Scots stood to lose
1 An Act of Union turning England and Scotland into a United Kingdom of Great Britain	Some Scots would gain more power and wealth, serving the new British Government in London	Their independence as a kingdom after hundreds of years
2 A single Parliament for England and Scotland in London	Some Scots would serve as MPs and Lords in the London Parliament	Their own Parliament, with power to pass its own laws
3 Freedom for Scottish merchants to trade in England, Ireland, and other settlements abroad	Some Scots might gain more wealth and power because they could trade freely and make more profits	Nothing
4 A British flag combining the old flags of England and Scotland	A new flag which included the old Scottish flag	Their own flag
5 Scottish control of their own Protestant Church, schools and courts	Scottish churchmen, teachers and lawyers would keep control in Scotland itself	Nothing
6 A single British Army and Royal Navy	Some Scots would gain from serving in the new Army and Navy	Their own army and navy

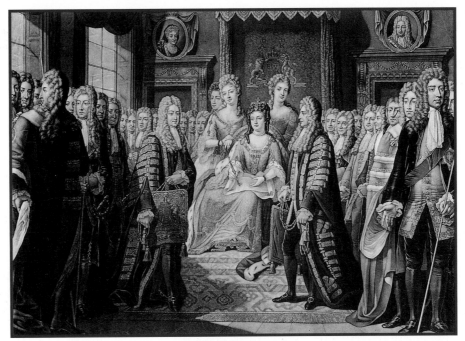

Queen Anne receives the Treaty of Union

In 1707, the English and Scottish Parliaments agreed to the Treaty of Union, and presented it to Queen Anne.

A new flag, the first version of the Union Jack, was created by putting together the old flags of England and Scotland. (Ireland was added in 1801.)

English cross of St George

Scottish cross of St Andrew

Union flag of Great Britain

In England, few people really cared about the Union with Scotland. Most thought of the new country of Great Britain as just a bigger version of England itself.

In Scotland, most people <u>hated</u> the Union. English politicians had bribed members of the Scottish Parliament to pass it, and threatened to invade Scotland if the Scots refused to agree. Scottish merchants hoped to do well from the deal. Scottish churchmen and lawyers were happy to keep control of their own affairs. Ordinary Scots were furious at their loss of independence. Anti-English feeling ran high.

Would this help or hinder the Jacobites?
In what way?

---

1 Look back at the events described on pages 78–81. Write out and fill in the chart below. Put a tick in the column which describes the effect of each event.

This would **help** the Jacobites		Events	This would **hinder** the Jacobites	
A lot	A bit		A lot	A bit
		1 Bank of England	✔	
		2 Act of Settlement		
		3 English victories		
		4 Treaty of Union		

2 Overall, did events between 1691 and 1714 help or hinder the Jacobites?

How close to success did the Jacobites come?

1 In 1714, Queen Anne died. She had no children, and her German cousin, George of Hanover, became King of Great Britain. This had been planned by Parliament as part of the Act of Settlement. James Stuart, the Catholic son of James II, was again overlooked. The new King was dull and hardly spoke any English. He brought with him two mistresses, a tall one nicknamed "The Maypole", and a fat one nicknamed "The Elephant". However, he was a Protestant and Parliament's choice.

Come and join my army. Long live King James VIII. Down with Hanover!

The Earl of Mar

I'm really annoyed. I wanted a job in King George's Government. Now I can't get one, I'll try King James instead.

2 Many Lords and politicians were unhappy with the new King and his Government. George listened to a group of advisers from Parliament called the Whigs. The King trusted only them. The Whigs excluded from power any of their old enemies. This included an important Scot – John, Earl of Mar. In 1715, he started a new Jacobite rebellion in Scotland to try and bring James's son to the throne.

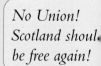

We want our own King! God save James VIII!

3 Many Scots agreed with Mar:

◆ They hated the Union and resented the English.

◆ They believed that, with James Stuart as their king, they would get back their independence and their own Parliament.

◆ In the Highlands, Mar's army gained support.

Perth

Edinburgh

No Union! Scotland shoul[d] be free again!

Down with the English!

4 Some Scots were not so sure:

◆ They distrusted Mar.

◆ They hated the idea of a Catholic King.

◆ They stayed loyal to King George I, who was a Protestant.

◆ Some cities in the Lowlands, like Edinburgh, also supported King George.

I don't like the English either, but we don't want a Catholic King!

Mar's nickname is "Bobbing John" because his ideas change so often. Why should we trust him now?

The ladders are too short! We need more rope!

By the time we've got more rope, the garrison will have spotted us.

5 Mar took decisions slowly, and the Jacobites made silly mistakes. They planned to capture Edinburgh Castle by climbing up the walls with rope ladders and surprising the garrison. The ladders were too short and while they were waiting for more rope, the soldiers in the garrison caught them.

Is this our King? He looks pathetic!

How cold and damp.

Peterhead

Sherrifmuir

Stirling

Preston

What scruffy Highlanders.

Devon

⚔ battle
☠ draw
✖ defeat

6 King George's soldiers captured Stirling Castle and blocked Mar's army in the Highlands. Mar fought a battle outside Stirling at Sherrifmuir, but it was a draw. That night, news reached the Jacobite camp that a small army of Jacobite rebels had been defeated at Preston. Mar's army, fed up and short of food and money, went home. A Jacobite attack on Devon also failed. The French sent no help. James Stuart himself then landed in Scotland but only stayed for six weeks before going back to France. He impressed no-one.

No wonder they call him "Mr Misfortune".

Rebellion 3: Scotland and England 1715

7 The rebellion was over. Mar fled to France. Soon after, James had to leave Paris for Rome, as George I reached new agreements with the French which meant they would no longer protect James. Some Jacobite lords were executed but Lord Nithsdale escaped from the Tower of London with his wife's help, disguised as a woman. This was the only cheerful news the Jacobites had.

I owe my life to my wife!

1 Write out this diagram under the heading **Rebellion 3: Scotland and England 1715**.

A strong army

Good leadership

Foreign help

SUCCESS

A weaker enemy

Luck

Popular support

Write a sentence or paragraph for each factor, to explain what happened in Scotland and England in 1715.

2 Now decide how close to success you think the Jacobites came with this third rebellion. Use the same scale as before:

1	2	3	4	5	6	7	8	9	10
Not close to success				Quite close to success					Very close to success

3 Explain in your own words who the Earl of Mar was and what he was fighting for.

1715–1745: Who needs the Stuarts?

James Stuart, son of James II, tried to invade Scotland again in 1719, this time with the support of Catholic Spanish troops. There was no rising, even in the Highlands. The attempt was a dismal failure.

James went back to Rome and concentrated on bringing up his young sons, Charles and Henry.

In the meantime, George I and his family became firmly established in both England and Scotland. General Wade was asked to build a very efficient system of roads and bridges across the Highlands, with the aim of moving Government redcoats swiftly in the event of another rebellion.

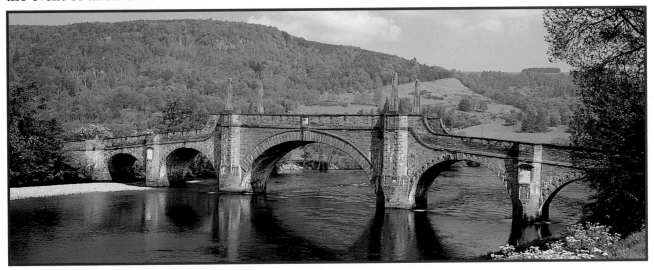

Wade's bridge at Aberfeldy

Neither George I (1714–1726) nor his son George II (1726–1760) were much liked. They were seen as dull and boring foreigners. But they were happy to trust the same small group of very wealthy families and their supporters to run the country. These families controlled Parliament, and for many years their leader was Britain's first Prime Minister, Sir Robert Walpole.

Trade increased and wealth flowed into Britain as British merchants struggled with the French to dominate North America and Indian trading posts. Many Scots also gained a cut of this wealth by trading or from Government jobs. For Britain's top families, life was sweet. Who needed the Stuarts? Who even remembered them?

One group of people did – the Jacobites. They were still trying to reclaim the throne for the Stuarts.

Did events from 1715 to 1745 help or hinder the Jacobites? If so, in what way?

The Duke of Newcastle, from one of the leading families

How close to success did the Jacobites come?

1 In 1744, Britain and France were at war again. King Louis XV of France sent to Rome for Prince Charles Edward Stuart (James's son), promising help for a new Jacobite rising. Just as an invasion fleet was ready to sail for England, it was wrecked by a storm. After this setback, the French lost interest.

2 Charles was disappointed, but he was a daring and spirited young man. Without the direct approval of his father, James Stuart, he sold some of his possessions and borrowed enough money to buy 1500 muskets, 1800 broadswords and some small cannon. He also hired two French ships, the "Elizabeth" and the "du Teillay", to carry himself and his weapons to Scotland. Without French help, he was gambling on being able to inspire Scots to join him in a new rebellion. His ships were swiftly attacked by the British Royal Navy and the one carrying all the weapons had to turn back. Charles landed in Scotland with just some supporters and nothing else.

The "Elizabeth" and "du Teillay" under attack from the British Navy

3 Charles called a secret meeting of Highland chiefs. Some either stayed at home or continued to support the Government of King George II. The chiefs that went to meet Charles doubted if they could achieve anything without French support. Charles inspired those chiefs with his personal charm. He also promised that French support was on its way and that Jacobites in England would rise up, too. The chiefs believed him, although he could not guarantee either promise. The Prince's standard was raised at Glenfinnan on 10th August, 1745.

Edinburgh

4 With white roses in their hats, and cries of "Long live King James" and "No Union", Prince Charles's army marched quickly south to Edinburgh (using General Wade's new road system). The City Council sent messengers to negotiate, but the Jacobites followed them back to the City gates and forced their way in.

5 By now, the Jacobites were in control of much of Scotland. They defeated a redcoat army at Prestonpans, thanks to the best Jacobite general, Lord George Murray. But the Prince decided not to take Edinburgh Castle. Instead, he marched south into England, hoping to pick up Jacobite volunteers and encourage the French to launch an invasion.

→ Jacobite advance

Edinburgh ✕ Prestonpans

Carlisle

Preston Manchester

Derby

6 A government army of redcoats planned to block the Jacobites' advance down the East coast of England. Instead, the Jacobites marched south down the West coast. In only five weeks, they reached Derby, just 127 miles from London. Terrified Londoners deserted the streets and hid their valuables but in Derby the chiefs decided by just one vote not to support an attack on London. Only 200 English volunteers had joined them. There was no news of French help. Although Prince Charles bitterly disagreed, the chiefs decided to return their 5000-strong army to Scotland.

Culloden

Dunkeld

→ **Jacobite retreat**

Falkirk

Carlisle

Preston

Manchester

7 More Scottish Jacobites joined them in the Highlands, and Lord George Murray defeated another Government army at Falkirk. However, the Prince's army still retreated and his advisers fell out more and more. Meanwhile, crack British troops had returned from the war with France to hunt the Jacobites down, led by the Duke of Cumberland.

8 Prince Charles had no money. The British Royal Navy stopped a French ship carrying gold for him. The Prince's Irish friends and the Highland chiefs quarrelled again. The Prince also fell out with his best general, Lord George Murray. The cold, hungry and tired Jacobites were outnumbered by a well-fed redcoat army under Cumberland at Culloden. At least a third of Cumberland's army were Scots.

On 16th April 1746, the Jacobites were finally defeated.
(Look back to pages 68–69 for the battle itself.)

What happened to the Jacobites?

Prince Charles Edward Stuart fled for his life. He escaped from the Highlands disguised as a maid. Returning to Rome, Charles never again posed a serious threat to the British Government. He died in 1788, a drunken womaniser. His brother, Prince Henry, the last Stuart prince, died in 1807.

But how close did the 1745 rebellion come to success?

---

1 Using the same headings as for the first three rebellions, decide how close you think the Jacobites came to success on their final attempt.

You are now going to look back at the four attempts the Jacobites made to regain power. This will help you to answer the question: **How close to success did the Jacobites come?**

2 Draw this living graph.

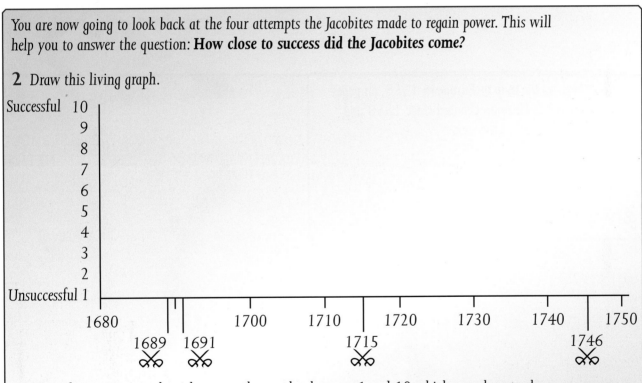

Now plot on your graph with a cross the number between 1 and 10 which you chose to show how close to success each of the four Jacobite rebellions were.

3 Use this writing frame to help you explain how close the Jacobites came to success.

In this essay, I am going to decide how close the Jacobites came to success.
I think they came closest to success in ...
This is because ... (You could mention examples of good luck, good leadership, a strong army, a weaker enemy, popular support, foreign help.)
I think they were least close to success in ...
This is because ... (Again, use examples to back up your decision.)
In conclusion, I think that ...

Europe in 1746

Culloden

1 Look back at the map of Europe in 1558, on pages 8–9. How has the map changed since 1558 and how has it remained the same?

2 Look at a modern map of Europe. What has changed since 1746 and what has remained the same?

3 Why do you think these changes have happened?

DUTC
REPUB

AUSTRIA
NETHERLA

FRANCE

SWITZERL

S.

PORTUGAL

SPAIN

REPUBLIC
OF GENOA

PARM

Minorca

Gibraltar

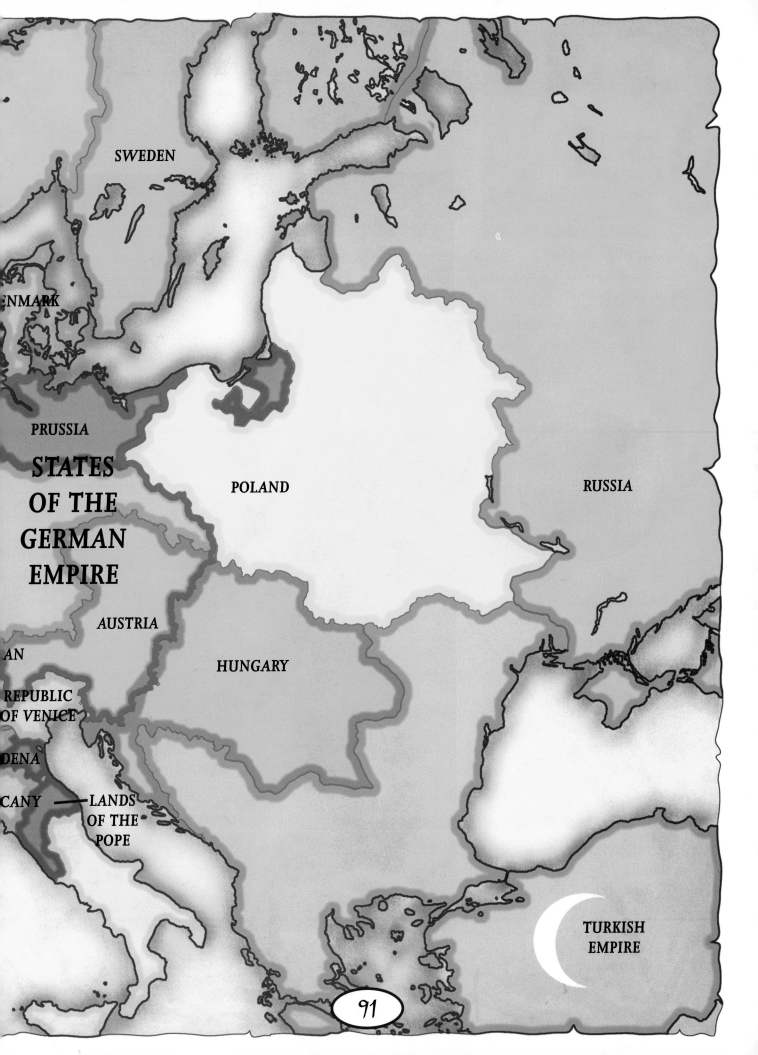

SWEDEN

ENMARK

PRUSSIA

**STATES
OF THE
GERMAN
EMPIRE**

AUSTRIA

AN

REPUBLIC
OF VENICE

DENA

CANY ——LANDS
OF THE
POPE

POLAND

HUNGARY

RUSSIA

TURKISH
EMPIRE

Portraits painted in the past can tell us a great deal about what the person being painted <u>wanted</u> to have shown about themselves. Often, they also contained 'hidden' messages, which aren't easy to understand.

This portrait was painted just after the defeat of the Spanish Armada in 1588, when Elizabeth I was 54.

The English fire ships attack the Spanish Armada off Calais, scattering the enemy fleet.

An **imperial** crown – Elizabeth is more than just Queen of England and Ireland. She commands the seas (in both good and bad weather) and the land (shown by the globe).

The Armada Portrait, 1588

The bad weather wrecks Spanish ships off the coast of Scotland and Ireland.

Elizabeth's hand rests on the globe, touching America. Not only do her sea captains raid treasure ships from Spanish America, she now has an English colony, Virginia (land of the Virgin), named after her.

Propaganda means using information to influence people. It is often exaggerated and sometimes untrue. Elizabeth used her portraits as propaganda, to make people think highly of her.

1 Look carefully at the details from the picture and read about what they mean.

2 You are the admirer of Elizabeth who asked the artist to paint this portrait. Write instructions telling him:

— what to include,
  e.g. the fire ships

— what **not** to include,
  e.g. the Queen's wrinkles

This portrait is called the Rainbow Portrait. It was painted in 1600, when Elizabeth was 66.

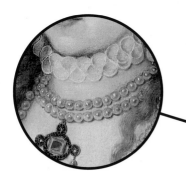

Elizabeth is wearing pearls. They are a symbol of her purity.

Elizabeth's dress is embroidered with English wild flowers. She is an English version of Flora, Goddess of Flowers.

ION SINE SOLE
IRIS.

The Rainbow Portrait, 1600

Elizabeth is wearing a crescent-shaped jewel. It shows she is also Cynthia, a goddess of the moon, Love and Beauty.

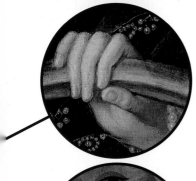

She is holding a rainbow with the motto *Non sine sole iris*, which means "No rainbow without the sun". The rainbow is a symbol of peace, and the motto means that there can be no rainbow, or peace, without the sun (Elizabeth).

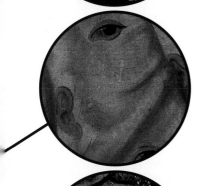

Eyes and ears cover her dress. This shows that Elizabeth is wise and intelligent, listening carefully to her many good advisers. She misses nothing because she has so many people looking and listening for her.

A serpent coils along her sleeve, dangling a heart-shaped ruby from its mouth. The serpent is a symbol of wisdom, surrounding the Queen's heart.

1 Look carefully at the details from the picture and what they mean.

2 You are an adviser in the same way as for the previous portrait. Write instructions telling the painter:
  — what to include in the picture, e.g. the Queens pearls
  — what <u>not</u> to include, e.g. the true colour of the Queen's hair (by this time she wore a wig over what little hair she had left)
  — your reasons for showing the Queen this way.

3 Compare your set of instructions for the painting of 1588 with the painting of 1600. How different are they?

Can you suggest why this is?

Powerful people try to control images of themselves. They want people to see them in a certain way. This is especially true about a queen, like Elizabeth. Few of her subjects ever actually saw her. Before photographs, television, radio, newspapers or the internet existed, people had to rely on paintings to know what the Queen looked like. They could see the Queen's picture on a coin, but the best images were kept by the richest people in the grandest houses.

This portrait of Elizabeth in her coronation robes was painted in 1559, when she was still young.

◆ Although her face is covered with milky-white make-up, it has no wrinkles.

◆ The red hair that cascades off Elizabeth's shoulders is her own, in its natural colour.

◆ The painting is stiff and formal, but probably reasonably true to life.

This picture was painted by Isaac Oliver in about 1593. The Queen strictly controlled the image on which all paintings had to be based. Any paintings she didn't approve of were burned. This picture was supposed to be a new official image. Elizabeth <u>hated</u> it.

◆ It showed that she was **old**.

◆ It showed that she had **wrinkles**.

◆ It showed that she wore a **wig**.

Look back at the Rainbow Portrait. What would this have looked like if the artist had used Isaac Oliver's painting as a basis for what he painted?

So how can we explain this portrait?

Two children float above the Queen, holding her crown. This symbolises two angels supporting the Queen's crown, showing she rules with God's blessing.

The skeleton peers over Elizabeth's shoulder with an hour glass. Death awaits the weary Queen, as the sands of time in the hour glass run out. (An hour glass was a bit like an egg timer.)

Elizabeth's dress is sewn with pearls and diamonds. (Diamonds were painted as if they were black.) The Queen still uses symbols of purity (pearls) and life (diamonds) – but how much time has she got left?

An old man holding a **scythe**, a tool used for cutting down crops and long grass. He represents Death, waiting to cut short the Queen's life.

The portrait was dated by experts to **about 1610**. Elizabeth died in **1603**. The experts dated the dress in the painting to one in fashion in 1610, <u>not</u> 1603 or before. It is very unlikely Elizabeth could have worn this dress in her lifetime. So, if there are problems trusting any image of Elizabeth, how can we be certain of what she looked like?

The answer is that we **can't be certain** but we can decide which portrait might be the **most realistic**. What do <u>you</u> think?

What evidence could we find from the portrait itself to back up the claim that it was painted well after Elizabeth's death? Use the questions below to help you answer this.

1 *What does the Queen's face look like? (Look at her expression, her complexion, her eyes.)*

2 *How is she sitting? (Look at her position, her pose and her posture.)*

3 *What sort of symbols surround her? (Can you see any symbols of power, wisdom or purity?)*

4 *Why is it unlikely that this portrait was painted in the Queen's lifetime?*

Can we use modern films as historical evidence?

The film *Elizabeth* was made in 1998. It was supposed to be about the early years of her reign. The film makers wanted it to be an exciting thriller about **love** and **power**. (Some scenes might upset younger children.)

The film opens with three Protestants burning as heretics on the orders of Mary I, Elizabeth's sister. It is meant to show how badly Catholics treated innocent Protestants. Elizabeth was also a Protestant.

FACT Mary ordered over 200 Protestants to be burned as heretics.

The film shows Elizabeth on her throne at her coronation.

FACT The film makers carefully based the costume on Elizabeth's coronation portrait. Many of the film's costumes were based on paintings from the time.

The film shows Elizabeth's relationship with Lord Robert Dudley. She has an affair with him, but he plots with the Spanish against her. She lets him live, as a constant reminder of his treachery.

FACT While she probably did love him, there is no evidence Elizabeth ever had an affair with Dudley. They sometimes quarrelled, but he was never a traitor. He served her loyally until his death in 1588.

One of the villains in the film is Sir Francis Walsingham. He is presented as the evil genius who destroys Elizabeth's enemies. He has an affair with the mother of Mary Queen of Scots, Elizabeth's cousin, and murders her. He also has old Bishop Gardiner killed. Another villain in the film is the Pope. He encourages Catholics to murder Elizabeth and sends a priest to do this.

FACT **Sir Francis was Elizabeth's ruthless and effective spy chief. However, he never had an affair with or murdered the mother of Mary Queen of Scots. Nor did he kill Bishop Gardiner – Gardiner died in his bed in 1555, before Elizabeth even became Queen. The Pope did cut off Elizabeth from the Catholic Church in 1571 and declared her to be no longer Queen. While there were plots by Catholics against Elizabeth's life, they were not ordered by the Pope.**

Sir William Cecil (Lord Burghley) is a wise adviser to the Queen. She retires him in favour of Walsingham.

FACT **Cecil worked closely with Walsingham all his life. The Queen never dismissed him.**

---

1 The film squeezes events from about 1554 to 1572 (eighteen years) into about six years (1554–1560). If all other evidence about Elizabeth was destroyed, what impression might a future historian get from this film, of:

a) her character?

b) her appearance?

c) the early events of her reign?

d) Catholics of Elizabeth's time?

... Can we use modern films as historical evidence?

The film *Shakespeare in Love* was made in 1998. It is a fictional story about the writer William Shakespeare. Although it is made up, some of the characters were real, and some details are accurate. It is set in the 1590s, when Elizabeth was an old woman. She is in the film for only nine minutes. The film makers wanted the film to be exciting but also **romantic** and **funny**. It can be seen by all the family.

Elizabeth goes to see one of Shakespeare's plays but then falls asleep during the performance. She is wearing a wig, and her white make-up does not hide her wrinkles.

FACT **This story line is made up, but the costume, wig and make-up are based on paintings and eye-witness accounts.**

Elizabeth is introduced to some leading characters. She makes witty and intelligent comments to them.

FACT **This is also made up. However, Elizabeth was a very intelligent woman, with a sharp tongue.**

Elizabeth visits a London theatre for the first performance of Romeo and Juliet by William Shakespeare.

FACT **Although the Queen watched plays at court, she did not go to ordinary theatres. However, she did watch plays by Shakespeare.**

1 If <u>all other evidence</u> about Elizabeth was destroyed, what impression might a future historian get from the film *Shakespeare in Love*, of:

a) her character?

b) her appearance?

c) the events of her reign?

Both *Elizabeth* and *Shakespeare in Love* give us some historical evidence about Elizabeth but, as we have seen, they are a mixture of fact and fiction. You would therefore have to be very careful about using any of the contents as a historical source. Perhaps these films are more useful as evidence of what some people think about Elizabeth <u>now</u>.

Elizabeth casts the Queen as a young heroine – not perfect, but very brave in protecting her throne from wicked Catholics.

Shakespeare in Love casts the Queen as a sharp and witty old woman with a strong sense of humour.

So, although the **purpose** of each film is different, they both cast Elizabeth in a good light.

2 Plan a modern film about Elizabeth, using a storyboard like the one below. Unlike the two films we have looked at, it must be critical and **negative** about her. It must favour the Catholics of the time and Elizabeth's other enemies. It must be an exciting thriller about **hatred** and **power**.

First, choose a title. Then look back at the sections in this book on Elizabeth. You will find the sections on the Church, the Catholics and the Armada important.

Choose six scenes to include in your storyboard. Draw each scene and write about it. Decide the kind of music and costumes you would use, and some dialogue too.

Portraits of Elizabeth I painted during, or just after, her lifetime, can tell us a lot about her and about what the artist wanted us to think about her. Films which are made a long time after her death can also tell us <u>something</u> about her – but they tell us <u>more</u> about what modern film makers want us to think about her.

Museums and historians give us a great deal of information about the past. They are not presenting us with fiction, as a film maker might do, but they do have to make a **selection** about what they are going to show us or tell us.

Frances Sword with a group of young visitors to the museum

❝My name is Frances Sword. I work at the Fitzwilliam Museum in Cambridge. Our museum has been loaned 20 pictures of the period 1500–1750 from important national collections.

We need to make plans for a travelling exhibition called **Macaulay's Country 1500–1750**. Thomas Babington Macaulay was a famous historian who wrote a history of England in the middle of Queen Victoria's reign.

We need to choose 10 paintings out of the 20 which we think Macaulay would have chosen himself. To help us make our decision, first read Macaulay's ideas below, and his views opposite about some of the things that happened between 1500 and 1750.❞

❝My name is Thomas Babington Macaulay. I believe in the greatness of England. Our empire stretches around the world. Wherever the Union Jack flies, fair play and common sense rule. We British have always loved freedom. Our Parliament at Westminster is the envy of the world. My bestselling book *History of England* shows how we have got to this position.❞

Macaulay's views

"
- Henry VIII and Queen Elizabeth freed the nation from the chains of the Roman Catholic religion.

- They set up our own moderate and sensible Church of England. It is Protestant but not extreme.

- England from that time was independent of Catholic Europe.

- In 1642, Parliament defended the nation's rights against the tyranny of Charles I.

- Oliver Cromwell, our greatest ever leader, led the nation to victory on land and sea.

- In 1688 William of Orange overthrew the Catholic tyrant, James II, and agreed to rule through Parliament.

- Our destiny as a great nation began.
"

1 From what you have read, do you think Macaulay was more sympathetic to Protestants or Catholics? What were his views of Parliament?

2 Look carefully at the 20 pictures shown on pages 104–108, and read the descriptions.

3 Decide which ten pictures you think should be chosen for **Macaulay's Country 1500–1750**.

4 Write a sentence in green describing each picture you have chosen, e.g.
This picture shows Protestants burning at the stake on the orders of Mary I.

5 Write a sentence or two in red describing the picture from Macaulay's point of veiw, e.g.
This picture shows how cruel Catholic Queen Mary burned innocent Protestants for their beliefs. It proves how wise Henry VIII and Elizabeth I were in making England Protestant.

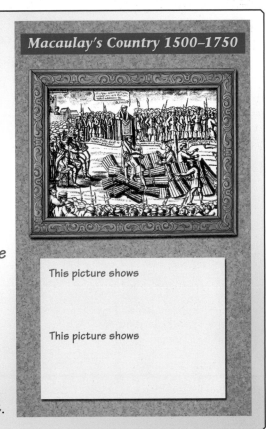

Macaulay's Country 1500–1750

This picture shows

This picture shows

The picture gallery

Henry VIII: Married six times. He broke with the Roman Catholic Church and set up a Protestant Church of England.

Protestant propaganda: Protestants being burned at the stake on the orders of Mary I. More than 200 Protestants were killed in this way by the Catholic Mary.

Henry VIII (1509–1547)	Edward VI (1547–1553)	M (155...

A black trumpeter from Henry VIII's court: Little is known about him except his name, John White. There were very few black people in Britain at the time.

The Armada Portrait of Elizabeth: This is propaganda celebrating the defeat of the Spanish Armada in 1588. Elizabeth set up a Protestant Church of England and executed about 150 Catholics, including Mary Queen of Scots.

Elizabeth I: A portrait completed in 1593 and intended to be a common pattern for other portraits. Elizabeth disliked it. It did not flatter her enough.

Catholic propaganda: A woodcut showing Edmund Campion being put to death on the orders of Elizabeth. While many Catholics were innocent of plotting against Elizabeth, some were guilty or were tricked into a plot by Walsingham, the Queen's spy chief.

Elizabeth I
(1558–1603)

Edmund Campion: A keen young Catholic priest sent to England in Elizabeth's reign. He was caught and tortured. Turning down Elizabeth's attempts to make him a Protestant, he was executed on fake charges of treason. The Roman Catholic Church called him a saint.

The Cobham Family: This portrait shows the wealthy family of Lord Cobham from the reign of Elizabeth I.

... The picture gallery

A woodcut showing three types of beggar from the reign of Elizabeth I: Rising prices and more and more people being born combined with bad harvests to take many more poor people into begging.

John Lilburne: He was the leader of a group of Puritans who wanted to make people more and more equal – to 'level' them. The Levellers demanded equal rights and votes for all men and women. They quarrelled with Cromwell and Parliament. Lilburne supported a serious mutiny among Cromwell's soldiers. He was put in prison and died there.

| James I (and VI of Scotland) (1603–1625) | Charles I (1625–1649) |

Charles I: This portrait is propaganda showing a powerful, larger-than-life King. It was painted by Van Dyck, Charles's court painter.

Oliver Cromwell: Member of Parliament, army general and Lord Protector of England, Scotland and Ireland (1653-1658). This is an official portrait but Cromwell insisted on being painted 'warts and all'.

Drogheda, Ireland, 1649: According to some historians, Cromwell's soldiers massacred the defenders of the town in cold blood.

James II of England and Ireland, James VII of Scotland: James was a Catholic who tried to get more tolerance for Catholics and Puritans. Many Protestants feared a Catholic take-over and James was overthrown by his son-in-law, William of Orange.

(Republic) 560)	Charles II (1660–1685)	James II (1685–1689)	William III (1689–1702) Mary II (1689–1694)

Charles II: Charles was 'restored' to the throne in 1660. He tried to avoid quarrels with Parliament and ended up relying on the Catholic King of France for money.

William III: William overthrew the Catholic James II peacefully in England. This was known as the Glorious Revolution, because it changed the King without having a civil war. But, William's armies had to defeat James's supporters by force in Scotland and Ireland. This propaganda portrait shows the defeat of James's supporters by William at the Battle of the Boyne in 1690.

... The picture gallery

A rich lady with her black servant: This was very fashionable late in the 17th century. There were still only a few black people in Britain, but many thousands of Africans were being shipped to British colonies in North America and the Caribbean to work as slaves. This boy's life would probably have been easier than theirs.

Designs for the Union flag: These flags put together the single flags of St George's red cross for England and St Andrew's blue cross for Scotland. The designs were drawn for James VI of Scotland when he became King of England and Ireland too. The real Union flag became the flag of the new United Kingdom when Scotland and England finally united in 1707.

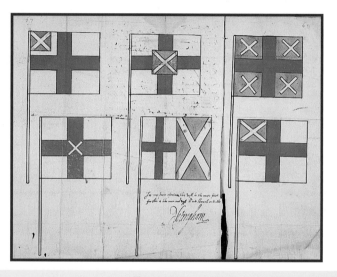

Anne (1702–1714)	George I (1714–1727)	George II (1727–1760)

Prince Charles Edward Stuart (1720–1788): Charles Stuart was the grandson of James II and is sometimes known as Bonnie Prince Charlie. He was a Catholic who led a Scottish Highland rebellion against King George II. The rebellion failed.

Mr and Mrs Andrews (1749): This portrait shows a rich young squire and his new bride. They stand on farmland where the fields have been enclosed and new farming techniques introduced. The couple probably married because both of their families were rich, not because they loved each other.

Frances Sword now has to prepare a second exhibition, this time from the point of view of the modern historian, Norman Davies. He wrote a book called *The Isles*, published in 1999.

"My name is Norman Davies. My job is to make sure people today understand their history properly. The country we call Britain may not exist much longer. Scotland and Wales have their own parliaments now. They may become independent. The British Empire has long gone. The monarchy may go the same way. We are a country of many faiths. My book shows us how we got here:

- Henry VIII and Elizabeth I cut England off from Europe by setting up the Church of England. They encouraged the English to look inward and distrust foreigners.

- The Civil War was a terrible conflict that involved people in Scotland, Ireland and Wales, not just England.

- Oliver Cromwell was a good general but he used force to conquer Scotland and Ireland. All male defenders were killed at Drogheda and Wexford. Civilians also died at Wexford.

- James II often said and did the wrong thing at the wrong time. However, he did try to persuade Protestants to become more tolerant.

- Britain is not the same as England. British history only began in 1707, when England forced Scotland into a United Kingdom of Great Britain. From 1801 it included Ireland.

- Our history is too dominated by the history of England. More space should be given to the histories of Scotland, Wales and Ireland. It only seems that these countries were certain to become united with England <u>after</u> it had all happened."

---

1 Decide which ten pictures you think should be chosen for **Davies's Country 1500–1750**. Then write a sentence in green describing each picture, as before, and a sentence in red describing the picture from Davies's point of view.

2 Which ten pictures would **you** choose to represent your views of Britain 1500–1750, and why?

3 Which collection of pictures do you think tells the truest story about the country from 1500–1750? Explain your answer.

Acknowledgements

Every effort has been made to contact the holders of copyright material but if any have been inadvertently overlooked the Publishers will be pleased to make the necessary arrangements at the first opportunity.

Extract on pages 57–58 adapted from 'O Horrable Murder' by Robert Partridge published by Rubicon Press in 1998.

Photographs

The Publishers would like to thank the following for permission to reproduce photographs on these pages:

T = top, B = bottom, C = centre, L = left, R = right

Art Directors/H. Rogers, 103; Courtesy of the Ashmolean Museum, Oxford, 55; Bank of England Museum© the Governor and Company of the Bank of England, 78T, 78B; Bibliotaca Nacional Madrid, 26–27; Bridgeman Art Library, London, 5T, 5B, 5B, 16T, 17T, 20C, 20B, 22, 67T, 68T, 71B, 86T, 96T, 105BR, 106BR, 108BL; Central Catholic Library, Dublin, 62T; College of Arms, London, 104BL; Corsham Court Collection, 97; The Cromwell Museum, Huntingdon, 60, 66R; © EMPICS/Steve Etherington, 47; *Felipe II*, Antonio Hernández Palacios (text and illustrations)/© Grupo Pandora, S.A. / Sociedad Estatal para la Conmemoración de los Centenarios de Felipe II y Carlos V, 31–33; Fotomas Index UK, 36, 37T, 37C, 61, 94–95, 106TL, 106TR; © Fitzwilliam Museum, Cambridge, 102T; Jeremy Walker/Getty Images, London, 98T; Collection of the Marquess of Salisbury at Hatfield House, 94–95; Hulton Archive, London, 62L, 81T, 107TL; The Kobal Collection, London, 42R, 98C, 98B, 99T, 99B, 100T, 100C, 100B; Macmillan Publishers Ltd, London, 109; Mary Evans Picture Library, London, 15TL, 41C, 85B, 102B; Metropolitan Museum of Art, Fletcher Fund 1933 (33.92b), Photograph © 1998, Metropolitan Museum of Art, 16B; Courtesy of the Director, National Army Museum, London, 75, 107BR; Van Dyck, Charles I/National Gallery, London, 106BL, Gainsborough, Mr & Mrs Andrews/National Gallery, London, 108BR; Trustees of the National Libraries of Scotland (MS2517), 108TL; National Museum, Stockholm, 15TR; National Portrait Gallery, London, 5C, 5C, 14T, 15BL, 15BR, 20T, 24T, 41TL, 41BR, 67TL, 71T, 79, 104TL, 105TR, 105BL, 107TR, 107BL; Reproduced by kind permission of The National Trust for Scotland, 63, 86B; Fran Caffrey/Newsfile, Ireland, 64; Patrimonio Nacional Madrid (Spain), 26, 27R; Pictures of Britain/R.V. Jones, 36–37; Rex Features Limited, 104TR; The Royal Collection © 2001, Her Majesty Queen Elizabeth II, 14B, 42L, 67C, 67B, 68–69 detail, 69T, 88B; Scottish National Portrait Gallery/Unknown, Henry Stuart Lord Darnley, 44TR; Scottish National Portrait Gallery/Paton, John Graham of Claverhouse, 77TL; Edwin Smith, 66L; © Pinhole Productions/Still Moving Picture Company, Edinburgh, 77; © Angus Johnson/Still Moving Picture Company, Edinburgh, 85T; V&A Picture Library, London, 12–13, 96B, 105TL, 108TR; West Highland Museum, Fort William, © R. Matassa, 70; Woburn Abbey, by kind permission of the Marquess of Tavistock and the Trustees of the Bedford Estate, 38, 92–93, 104BR.

Artwork

The Publishers would like to thank the following for permission to reproduce artwork on these pages:

Hodder Wayland/Richard Hook, 87T; Artwork from *'The Jacobite Rebellions'*, by Gerry Embleton © Osprey Publishing Ltd, 76.

All other artwork by Peter Bull

Index

Index